WOUNDED KNEE

OTHER BOOKS BY DEE BROWN

The Year of the Century: 1876
The Galvanized Yankees
Action at Beecher Island
Grierson's Raid
The Girl from Fort Wicked
Pawnee, Blackfoot, and Cheyenne;
History and Folklore of the Plains,
from the Writings of George Bird Grinnell
Fort Phil Kearny: An American Saga
The Gentle Tamers
The Bold Cavaliers
Yellowhorse
Bury My Heart at Wounded Knee:
An Indian History of the American West
The Westerners

WITH MARTIN F. SCHMITT

The Fighting Indians of the West
The Settlers' West
Trail Driving Days

Dee Brown

WOUNDED KNEE

AN INDIAN HISTORY OF THE AMERICAN WEST

Adapted for young readers by AMY EHRLICH
from Dee Brown's *Bury My Heart at Wounded Knee*

Holt, Rinehart and Winston
New York   Chicago   San Francisco

For

Nicolas Brave Wolf

Copyright © 1974 by Holt, Rinehart and Winston, Inc.
Copyright © 1970 by Dee Brown

All rights reserved, including the right to reproduce this
book or portions thereof in any form.

Published simultaneously in Canada by Holt, Rinehart and
Winston of Canada, Limited.

Library of Congress Cataloging in Publication Data
Ehrlich, Amy, date
Wounded Knee; an Indian history of the American West.
SUMMARY: Traces the white man's conquest of the
Indians of the American West, emphasizing the causes,
events, and effects of the major Indian Wars leading
to the symbolic end of Indian freedom at Wounded Knee.
Includes bibliographical references.
1. Indians of North America—The West—Wars—
Juvenile literature. 2. The West—History—Juvenile
literature. [1. Indians of North America—Wars.
2. The West—History] I. Brown, Dee Alexander. Bury
my heart at Wounded Knee. II. Title.
E81.E45   970.5   73-21821
ISBN 0-03-091559-7

Designed by Sandra Kandrac
33, and 153 by Jack Fuller
65 by Susan Scher

ted States of America
7 6 5 4 3 2

12545

Contents

List of Illustrations

Frontispiece: A Navaho warrior of the 1860's.
Photographed by John Gaw Meem and reproduced
by permission of the Denver Art Museum.

Preface

IN OUR MANY STORIES of the American West, the voices of
Indians have seldom been heard. Until after they were defeated and driven upon reservations, few Indians knew how
to write or read the language of their conquerors. The Plains
tribes kept pictographic records known as calendars or winter
counts, but not many of these records survived the destruc-
tive wars waged against the Indians by white men. Indian
history was preserved mainly through the spoken word told
by fathers and mothers to their sons and daughters who in
turn passed it on to their children.

Once in a while an Indian who had learned English would
write down an incident of tribal history. Sometimes a sympathetic white person or an enterprising newspaper reporter
would interview survivors of the Indian Wars, and these bits
of history would be printed in newspapers or magazines or
books. Much Indian history, told in the words of Indians
themselves, can be found in records of treaty councils. These
councils were held during the years when white people were
invading the Great Plains and other areas of the West where
tribes had lived for thousands of years. Because these meetings were between leaders of Indian tribes and representatives of the United States government, an official record was
kept in writing. Whenever an Indian spoke, his words were
translated into English by an interpreter and written down
by a recording clerk.

At the treaty meetings, most Indians spoke with deep feelings about their history, their land which the white invaders wanted to take from them, and of the important relationship of animals, plants, streams, air, sky, and earth to mankind. Although the Indians who lived in that time have long ago vanished from the earth, their words are preserved in these official records.

This book is the story of the American West told from these various sources of Indian history. Whenever possible, the story is told in the words of Indians who were there when it happened. Americans who have always looked westward when reading of the so-called winning of the West should read this book facing eastward. That was the direction the Plains Indians were facing as these terrible events in their history unfolded.

Those who read this story of American Indians of the past will better understand American Indians of today. History never dies. It flows through time and becomes a part of us. Only by knowing what happened at Wounded Knee in 1890 can we understand what happened at Wounded Knee in 1973.

D.B.

Introduction

IT BEGAN when Christopher Columbus landed on the island of San Salvador in the West Indies. He called the people who lived there *Indios*. As was their custom, the Taino Indians of San Salvador gave Columbus and his men gifts and treated them with honor.

"So tractable, so peaceful are these people," Columbus wrote to the King and Queen of Spain, "that I swear to your Majesties, there is not in the world a better nation. They love their neighbors as themselves and their discourse is ever sweet and gentle, and accompanied with a smile; and though it is true that they are naked, yet their manners are decorous and praiseworthy."

All this, of course, was taken as a sign of heathen weakness. Columbus felt that the people should be "made to work, sow, and do all that is necessary and to *adopt our ways*." Over the next four centuries (1492–1890) several million Europeans arrived to force their ways upon the Indians of the New World.

The Tainos and other Arawak people of the West Indies were willing to convert to the Europeans' religion but when these bearded strangers began to trample their islands in search of gold and precious stones, they resisted. The Spaniards looted and burned villages; they kidnapped hundreds of men, women, and children and shipped them back to Europe to be sold as slaves. Because the Spaniards used guns and sabers in battle, the Tainos were helpless against them. In less than ten years after Columbus set foot on the beach of San Salvador, whole tribes were destroyed, hundreds of thousands of people.

The English-speaking white men who arrived in Virginia in 1607 did not find the Powhatan tribe as welcoming as the Tainos had been. To make certain peace lasted long enough to start a settlement at Jamestown, the Englishmen crowned Wahunsonacook King Powhatan and convinced him to put his people to work supplying the white settlers with food. Wahunsonacook remained loyal to the British, especially after his daughter, Pocahontas, married John Rolfe. When Wahunsonacook died, however, the rebellious Powhatans rose up in revenge to drive the Englishmen back into the sea from which they had come. The Indians underestimated the power of English weapons. In a short time eight thousand Powhatans were reduced to less than a thousand.

In Massachusetts the story began differently but ended much the same. Most of the Englishmen who came to Plymouth in 1620 probably would have starved to death if not for the help of friendly Indians. Samoset, a Pemaquid, and three Wampanoags shared corn with the Pilgrims. They also showed them where and how to catch fish and in general helped them through the first winter.

For several years these Englishmen and their Indian neighbors lived in peace. But shiploads of white people continued to arrive, and settlements began crowding in upon each other. In 1625 some colonists asked Samoset for twelve thousand more acres of Pemaquid land. Samoset knew that land came from the Great Spirit, that it was as endless as the sky, and belonged to no man. To humor these strangers in their strange ways, however, he made his mark on a piece of paper for them. This was the first deed of Indian land to English colonists.

Most of the other settlers, coming by the thousands now, did not bother to go through such a ceremony. They merely took what land they wanted. By the 1660s the Wampanoags were being pushed back into the wilderness. A chief named Metacom believed the Indians were doomed unless they united to resist the invaders. Accordingly, he began to form alliances with the Narragansetts and other tribes in the region.

In 1675, Metacom led his Indian confederacy in a war against the colonists. The Indians attacked fifty-two settlements, completely destroying twelve of them. But after months of fighting, the firepower of the colonists nearly exterminated the tribes. Metacom was killed and his head exhibited at Plymouth for twenty years. His father had been Massasoit, great chief of the Wampanoags, one of the four Indians who had kept the first colonists alive in the New World.

When the Dutch came to Manhattan Island, Peter Minuit bought it for sixty guilders in fishhooks and glass beads, but encouraged the Indians to remain. Then in 1641, Willem Kieft sent soldiers to Staten Island to punish the Raritan Indians for crimes that had actually been committed by white settlers. The Raritans resisted arrest and the soldiers killed four of them. When the Indians retaliated by killing four Dutchmen, Kieft ordered the massacre of two entire villages while the people slept. The Dutch soldiers ran their bayonets through men, women, and children, hacked their bodies to pieces, and then set the villages on fire.

For two more centuries such events were repeated again and again as the European colonists moved inland, always searching for new land to develop. The Iroquois, the Ottawas, the Shawnees, and most of the other tribes that stood in the way were reduced or destroyed by the deadly weapons of the invading white men.

Yet even as late as the 1830s there were areas in the Southeast that the settlers could not easily take over. The Cherokees, Chickasaws, Choctaws, Creeks, and Seminoles were still numerous. They clung to their tribal lands which had been assigned them forever by white men's treaties. The United States Congress, under Andrew Jackson, then passed *An Act to Regulate Trade and Intercourse with the Indian Tribes and to Preserve Peace on the Frontiers*. Under this law the eastern tribes were all to be transported beyond the Mississippi River and given a vast land area.

Before the law could be put into effect, however, many more white settlers came westward and forced the policy makers in Washington to shift the "permanent Indian frontier" from the Mississippi to the 95th meridian. (This line ran from Lake of the Woods on what is now the Minnesota-Canada border southward to Galveston Bay, Texas.) No white people could settle in the Indian country. No white people could trade with the Indians without a license. Soldiers would be posted along the boundary to "protect" the Indians. In all this legislation, of course, not a single Indian had been consulted.

More than three centuries had now passed since Columbus had landed on San Salvador, more than two centuries since the English colonists came to Virginia and New England. In that time the friendly Tainos who had welcomed Columbus ashore had been completely wiped out. Long before the last of the Tainos died, their simple agriculture was replaced by cotton plantations worked by slaves. When Columbus first saw the island he described it as "very big and very level and the trees very green . . . the whole of it so green that it is a pleasure to gaze upon." The Europeans who followed him there destroyed its vegetation and its inhabitants—human, animal, bird, and fish. After turning it into a wasteland they abandoned it.

On the mainland of America, the forests were quickly disappearing under the axes of twenty million invaders. Already the once sweet-watered streams were clouded with silt; the very earth was being ruined. The Indians knew that life was equated with the earth and its resources, that America was a paradise. It seemed to them that these Europeans hated everything in nature—the living forests and their birds and beasts, the water, the soil, and the air itself.

The ten years following establishment of the "permanent Indian frontier" was a bad time for the eastern tribes. The great Cherokee nation had survived more than a hundred years of the white man's war, diseases, and whiskey. Now it was to be blotted out. Because there were several thousand of them, their journey to the West was planned in gradual stages. But discovery of Appalachian gold in Cherokee territory brought on a demand for their immediate removal. Accordingly, they were rounded up by soldiers, put in prison camps, and then started westward to Indian Territory in the middle of winter. One of every four Cherokees died from cold, hunger, or disease. They called the march their "trail of tears." The Choctaws, Chickasaws, Creeks, and Seminoles also gave up their homelands in the South. In the North, survivors of the Shawnees, Miamis, Ottawas, Hurons, Delawares, and many other once mighty tribes walked or traveled by horseback and wagon beyond the Mississippi. They carried with them their shabby goods, their rusty farming tools, and their bags of seed corn. All of them arrived as refugees, poor relations, in the country of the proud and free Plains Indians.

The refugees had just settled beyond the "permanent Indian frontier" when soldiers began marching westward through the Indian country. The white men of the United States were going to war with the white men who had conquered the Indians of Mexico. When the war with Mexico ended in 1847, the United States had won a vast amount of territory reaching from Texas to California. All of it was west of the "permanent Indian frontier."

In 1848 gold was discovered in California. Soon white people in covered wagons were crossing through Indian Territory by the thousands. Most were fortune seekers bound for California gold, but some turned southwest for New Mexico or northwest for the Oregon country.

To justify these violations of the "permanent Indian frontier," the policy makers in Washington invented Manifest Destiny. This set forth the idea that the Europeans and their descendants were meant by destiny to rule all of America. They were the controlling race and therefore should be responsible for the Indians—along with their lands, their forests, and their mineral wealth.

Faster and faster, United States citizens came into Indian Territory to claim what they now felt belonged to them. In 1850 California became a state; in 1858 Minnesota became a state. During this same period, two vast new territories were organized, Kansas and Nebraska, which included almost all the country of the Plains tribes.

And so only twenty-five years after the passing of Andrew Jackson's Indian Trade and Intercourse Act, white settlers, miners, and traders had gone beyond the 95th meridian into the very center of Indian Territory.

In 1860 when the white man's Civil War began, there were probably three hundred thousand Indians in the United States and Territories. Their number had been reduced by more than one-half since the arrival of the first settlers. Most of the survivors now lived west of the Mississippi. Suddenly they found themselves pressed between expanding white populations in the east and along the Pacific Coast—more than thirty million Europeans and their descendants with an insatiable hunger for territory and the weapons to seize it.

Against such an enemy, the remaining free tribes did not have a chance. Yet they knew the tragedy of their eastern brothers. Once the white invaders took their land, their independence would be taken from them as well. What could they do but resist?

The Navahos and the Apaches of the Southwest and the huge tribes of the Great Plains—the Cheyennes and the Sioux—resisted with all their power, with their very lives, for as long as they had chiefs to lead them into battle. The names of these men—Cochise, Geronimo, Crazy Horse, Sitting Bull, and many more—have become part of history and legend. Most of them were destroyed long before the symbolic end of Indian freedom came at Wounded Knee in December 1890. Now, a century later, in an age without heroes, they are perhaps the most heroic of all Americans.

Part One

THE NAVAHOS AND THE APACHES:

TRIBES OF THE SOUTHWEST

1

The Long Walk of the Navahos

When our fathers lived they heard that the Americans were coming across the great river westward. . . . We heard of guns and powder and lead—first flintlocks, then percussion caps, and now repeating rifles. We first saw the Americans at Cottonwood Wash. We had wars with the Mexicans and the Pueblos. We captured mules from the Mexicans, and had many mules. The Americans came to trade with us. When the Americans first came we had a big dance, and they danced with our women. We also traded.

—MANUELITO OF THE NAVAHOS

THE NAVAHOS were a large tribe who lived in the dry and rugged country of the Southwest. Unlike most western Indians, they had been fighting Spanish-speaking white men for two hundred and fifty years before the Americans began to come into their territory.

By the 1850s, however, most Navahos had taken the Spanish white man's road and were leading a settled existence, cultivating the land and raising animals. Some bands of the tribe had grown wealthy as herdsmen and weavers. Other Navahos continued as nomads, raiding their old enemies the Pueblos, the Mexicans, or members of their own tribe.

When the troubles with the new English-speaking white

3

men began, Manuelito, a prosperous herdsman, was head chief. He had been chosen by an election of the Navahos held in 1855. Manuelito and other leaders made treaties with the Americans. "Then the soldiers built the fort here," Manuelito remembered, "and gave us an agent who advised us to behave well. He told us to live peaceably with the whites; to keep our promises. They wrote down the promises, so that we would always remember them."[1]

Manuelito tried to keep the promises in the treaty. But after the soldiers came and burned his hogans and killed his livestock because of something a few wild young Navahos had done, he grew angry at the Americans. He and his band had been wealthy, but the soldiers had made them poor. To become *ricos* again they must raid the Mexicans to the south. For as long as anyone could remember, the Mexicans had been raiding Navahos to steal their young children and make slaves of them. And for as long as anyone could remember the Navahos had been retaliating with raids against the Mexicans.

After the Americans came to Santa Fe and called the country New Mexico, they protected the Mexicans because they had become American citizens. The Navahos were not citizens because they were Indians. Whenever there were raids, soldiers would punish the Navahos for stealing from the Mexicans. No Mexicans were ever punished for stealing from Indians. It all seemed an angry puzzle to Manuelito and his people.

The first fort the Americans built in the Navaho country was in a grassy valley at the mouth of Canyon Bonito. They called it Fort Defiance, and put their horses out to graze on pastureland long prized by Manuelito's band. Because there were no fences, the Navahos' livestock strayed onto the pastures. One morning some soldiers rode out of the fort and shot all the animals belonging to the Navahos.

To replace their horses and mules, the Navahos raided the soldiers' herds. The soldiers in turn began to attack bands of Navahos. Finally Manuelito and his ally Barboncito built up a force of more than a thousand warriors and attacked Fort Defiance. They were determined to wipe it off the face of their land. They did not have adequate weapons to do so. But, by the time the Navahos pulled back into the hills they were satisfied they had at least taught the soldiers a good lesson.

The United States Army, however, considered the attack a challenge of the flag over Fort Defiance, an act of war. For a whole year soldiers led by Colonel Edward Canby chased Manuelito and his men through the Chuska Mountains but were unable to catch them. In January 1861, a meeting was held between Manuelito and other *rico* leaders and Colonel Canby. The Indians wanted to return to their crops and live-stock and readily signed a new peace treaty. This time they hoped to be left alone.

After the winter meeting there were several months of friendship between the soldiers and the Navahos. A second fort, called Fort Wingate, had been built and the Navahos went there often to trade. The custom started of having horse races between the Navahos and the soldiers. All the Navahos looked forward to these contests and on racing days hundreds of men, women, and children would dress in their brightest costumes and ride their finest ponies to Fort Wingate. One September morning there was a special race scheduled be-tween Manuelito and a soldier lieutenant. Their horses jumped off together but in a few seconds Manuelito lost con-trol of his pony and it ran off the track. Soon everyone could see that Manuelito's bridle rein had been slashed with a knife.

Angry at the trickery, the Navahos stormed after the judges —who were all soldiers—and demanded that the race be run again. The judges refused and slammed the fort's gates shut in their faces. When a Navaho tried to force his way in, he was shot dead. What happened next was written down by a white soldier chief:

> The Navahos, squaws, and children ran in all directions and were shot and bayoneted. . . . I saw a soldier murdering two little children and a woman. I hallooed immediately to the soldier to stop. He looked up, but did not obey my order. I ran up as quick as I could, but could not get there soon enough to prevent him from killing the two innocent children and wounding severely the squaw. . . . Meanwhile the colonel had given orders to the officer of the day to have the artillery brought out to open upon the Indians. . . . After the massacre there were no more Indians to be seen about the post with the exception of a few squaws. . . .[2]

That day was September 22, 1861. It was a long time before there was friendship again between white men and Navahos.

Rumors had been reaching the Indians of a big war somewhere to the east, a war between the Americans of the North and the South. At first it seemed to the Navahos that they were far away from the white man's Civil War. But in 1861 an army of Confederate Graycoats had marched into New Mexico and fought big battles with the Bluecoats along the Rio Grande. Kit Carson, the Rope Thrower, was a leader of the Bluecoats. Most of the Navahos knew of Rope Thrower Carson and trusted him because he had always talked truthfully to Indians. They hoped to make peace with him when he was finished with the Graycoats.

In the spring of 1862, however, many more Bluecoats came marching into New Mexico from the west. Their general, James Carleton, wore stars on his shoulders and was much more powerful than Carson. He and his men camped along

1. *Manuelito, chief of the Navahos, painted by Julian Scott for the United States Census Bureau in 1891.*

the Rio Grande Valley, but they had no one to fight because all the Graycoats had fled into Texas.

The Navahos soon learned that Star Chief Carleton had a great hunger for their land. "A princely realm," he called it, "a magnificent pastoral and mineral country." Since he could not find any Graycoat soldiers, he began looking around for Indians to fight. The Navahos, he said, were "wolves that run through the mountains" and had to be tracked down.

Star Chief Carleton had prepared the Bosque Redondo reservation on some worthless land far away in the Pecos. If all the Indians could be moved there, the territory which they occupied would be open for settlement by American citizens. In April 1863, Carleton arranged a meeting with several *rico* leaders. He told them that the only way they could prove they wanted peace would be to take their people to live on the reservation. To this Barboncito replied: "I will not go to the Bosque. I will never leave my country, not even if it means that I will be killed."

On June 23 Carleton set a deadline for surrender. Any Navahos who still refused to go to the Bosque Redondo by July 20 would be hunted down. July 20 came and went but no Indians volunteered to surrender.

In the meantime Carleton had ordered Kit Carson to march his troops to Fort Wingate to prepare for a war against the Navahos. Carson was reluctant. He had enlisted to fight Confederate soldiers, not Indians, and he tried to resign from the Army.

Kit Carson liked Indians. In his days as a trader he had lived with them for months without seeing another white man. But since then things had changed in New Mexico. Carson had discovered that there was room at the top even for a rough mountain man who could hardly read or write. The land he had claimed for a ranch and the respect of people like Carleton had come to mean more to him than old friendships with Indians. So in the summer of 1863 Carson withdrew his resignation and went to Fort Wingate to make war against the Navahos.

Though they respected Carson as a fighter, the Indians were unafraid. It was their land they were defending and they knew its every canyon, cliff, and mesa. Their stronghold was Canyon de Chelly. Cutting westward for thirty miles from the Chuska Mountains, the canyon had red rock walls that rose a thousand feet or more. At wide places inside the canyon, the Navahos grazed sheep and goats, or raised corn, wheat, fruit, and melons. They were especially proud of their peach orchards, carefully tended since the days of the Spaniards.

When they learned that Carson had over a thousand soldiers, the Navaho chiefs reminded their people of how in the old days they had driven the Spaniards from their land. "If the Americans come to take us, we will kill them," the chiefs promised.

Late in July Carson moved up to Fort Defiance, renamed it for the Indians' old enemy Canby, and began his campaign against the Navahos. He knew they would stay well hidden and that the only way to conquer them was to destroy their crops and livestock—to scorch their earth. But he did not move quickly enough for General Carleton. On August 18 the general decided to "stimulate the zeal" of his soldiers by offering money for every Navaho horse, mule, and sheep brought into Fort Canby.

Since the soldiers did not get paid very much, the bounty offer did stimulate them. Some of the men even extended it to the few Navahos they were able to kill. To prove their soldierly abilities, they began cutting off the knot of hair fastened by a red string which the Navahos wore. The Navahos could not believe that Kit Carson approved of scalping, which they considered a barbaric custom started by the Spaniards. (The Europeans may or may not have brought scalping to the New World, but the Spanish, French, Dutch, and English colonists made the custom popular by offering bounty money for the scalps of their enemies.)

Pushed by General Carleton, Carson accelerated his scorched-earth program. By autumn he had destroyed most of the herds and grain between Fort Canby and Canyon de Chelly. On October 17 two Navahos appeared under a truce flag at Fort Wingate. One of them was El Sordo, who had been sent by his brothers Delgadito and Barboncito and their five hundred followers. Their food supply was gone, El Sordo said; they had only piñon nuts to eat. They were almost without clothing and blankets, and too afraid of soldiers' hunting parties to build fires for warmth. They did not want to go far away to the Bosque, but would build hogans near Fort Wingate, where they would always be under the eyes of the soldiers as peaceful Indians.

But when the compromise offer was sent to General Carleton, he refused it. Under no conditions would he allow the Navahos to remain in their own country. A new gold strike had made it far too valuable. In a memo to the War Department asking for more soldiers, Carleton had clearly stated his intent "to whip the Indians and to protect the people going to and at the mines. . . . Providence has indeed blessed us . . . the gold lies here at our feet to be had by the mere picking of it up!"[3]

The Navahos who had offered to make peace were shown no mercy. They could either surrender and go to the Bosque Redondo or hold out, risking starvation, freezing, or death at the hands of Kit Carson's soldiers. Burdened with suffering women and children, Delgadito surrendered. Barboncito, El

Sordo, and many of the warriors waited in the mountains to see what would happen to their people.

It was then that General Carleton ordered Carson to invade Canyon de Chelly and kill or capture the Navahos there. After one false start the soldiers finally marched out of Fort Canby on January 6, 1864. Six inches of snow lay on the ground, the temperature was below freezing, and the journey was slow.

A week later the first group of soldiers entered the east end of the canyon. From rims and ledges hundreds of half-starved Navahos hurled stones, pieces of wood, and Spanish curses upon their heads. But they could not stop them. The soldiers marched straight through, burning hogans, destroying food supplies, capturing the women and children, and killing any Navahos who got within range of their guns. On January 14 they linked up with Carson's men who had made camp at the western end. The entire canyon had been taken without a major fight.

That evening three Navahos approached the soldiers under a truce flag. Their people were starving and freezing, they told Carson. They chose to surrender rather than die. "You have until tomorrow morning," Carson replied. "After that time my soldiers will hunt you down." Next morning, sixty starved and ragged Navahos arrived at the camp and surrendered.

Before returning to Fort Canby, Carson ordered complete destruction of everything the Navahos had grown in the Canyon—including their fine peach orchards, more than five thousand trees. The Navahos could forgive the Rope Thrower for fighting them as a soldier, even for making prisoners of them, but the one act they never forgave him for was cutting down their beloved peach trees.

During the next few weeks as news of the soldiers' victory

at Canyon de Chelly spread through the hidden camps of the Navahos, the people lost heart. "We fought for that country because we did not want to lose it," Manuelito said afterward. "We lost nearly everything. . . . The American nation is too powerful for us to fight. When we had to fight for a few days we felt fresh, but in a short time we were worn out and the soldiers starved us out."[4]

By early spring of 1864 three thousand had surrendered and come in to the two forts. They had been forced to do so because of the lack of food and severe winter weather, but conditions at the forts were no better. The army gave out only small amounts of food and the very old and the very young began to die.

During March, the Long Walk of the Navahos to the Bosque Redondo was set in motion. It took place in three stages. The Navahos had the strength to bear freezing weather, hunger, and the hard three-hundred-mile journey, but they could not bear the homesickness, the loss of their land. They wept and hundreds of them died before they reached their cruel destination.

An officer in command reported, "On the second day's march, a very severe snowstorm set in which lasted for four days with unusual severity, and occasioned great suffering amongst the Indians, many of whom were nearly naked and of course unable to withstand such a storm." This march reached the Bosque on May 11, 1864. "I left Fort Canby with 800 and received 146 en route . . . making about 946 in all. Of this number about 110 died."

Throughout that long hard winter, Manuelito and Barboncito had stayed with their people in the mountains, still determined not to surrender. Late in April Manuelito came out of hiding for a meeting with the commander of Fort Canby.

2. *Barboncito, photographer not recorded, but taken no later than 1870. Courtesy of the Smithsonian Institution.*

He told the soldier chief that his people wished to stay near the fort, plant their grain crops, and graze their sheep as they had always done.

"Why must we go to the Bosque?" Manuelito asked. "We have never stolen or murdered and have at all times kept the peace we promised General Canby." He added that his people feared they were being collected at the Bosque so soldiers could shoot them down as they had after the horse race at Fort Wingate in 1861. The soldier chief assured him that this was not so, but Manuelito said he would not surrender his people and disappeared once more.

In September he heard that his old ally Barboncito had been captured in the Canyon de Chelly. Now he, Manuelito, was the last of the *rico* holdouts, and he knew the soldiers would be looking everywhere for him.

During the autumn, Navahos who had escaped from the Bosque Redondo began returning to their homeland with frightening tales of what was happening to the people there. It was an ugly and barren land, they said. The soldiers pushed them with bayonets and herded them into adobe-walled areas where the soldiers were always counting them and putting numbers down in little books. The soldier chiefs promised them clothing and blankets and better food, but their promises were never kept. All the trees had been cut down so that only roots were left for firewood. To shelter themselves from rain and sun they had to dig holes in the sandy ground and cover them with mats of woven grass. They lived like prairie dogs in burrows. Because they were so crowded, disease had begun to strike down the weaker ones. It was a bad place, and although escape was difficult, many were risking their lives to get away.

Ignoring the Indians' suffering, Star Chief Carleton described the place to his superiors in Washington as "a fine reservation . . . there is no reason why they [the Navahos] will not be the most happy and prosperous and well-provided-for Indians in the United States. . . . At all events . . . we can feed them cheaper than we can fight them."

And no supporter of Manifest Destiny ever used that philosophy more smugly than he did:

> The exodus of this whole people from the land of their fathers is not only an interesting but a touching sight. They have fought us gallantly for years on years; they have defended their mountains and their stupendous canyons with a heroism which any people might be proud to emulate; but when, at length, they found it was their destiny, too, as it had been that of their brethren, tribe after tribe, away back toward the rising of the sun, to give way to the insatiable progress of our race, they threw down their arms, and, as brave men entitled to our admiration and respect . . . we will not dole out to them a miser's pittance in return for what they know to be and what we know to be a princely realm.[5]

Manuelito had not thrown down his arms, however, and he was too important a chief for General Carleton to ignore. In February 1865, Navaho runners brought Manuelito a message from the Star Chief, a warning that he and his band would be hunted to the death unless they came in peaceably before spring. "I am doing no harm to anyone," Manuelito told the messengers. "I will not leave my country. I intend to die here." But he finally agreed to talk with some of the chiefs who were at the Bosque Redondo.

In late February, six Navaho leaders were released from the Bosque to meet with Manuelito and propose the terms for his surrender. The weather was cold and the land was covered with deep snow. After embracing his old friends, Manuelito led them back into the hills where his people were hidden. Only about a hundred people were left of Manu-

elito's band; they had a few horses and a few sheep. "Here
is all I have in the world," Manuelito said. "See what a
trifling amount. You see how poor they are. My children are
eating palmilla roots." After a pause he added that his horses
could not travel to the Bosque just then. One of the Navaho
leaders, a man named Herrero Grande, replied that he had
no authority to extend the time for him to surrender. Manuelito wavered. He said he would surrender for the sake of the
women and children. Finally he declared flatly that he could
not leave his country.

"My God and my mother live in the West, and I will not
leave them. . . . Nor could I leave the Chuska Mountains. I
was born there. I shall remain. I have nothing to lose but my
life, and *that* they can come and take whenever they please,
but I will not move. I have never done any wrong to the
Americans or the Mexicans. I have never robbed. If I am
killed, innocent blood will be shed."

Herrero Grande said to him: "I have done all I could for
your benefit; have given you the best advice; I now leave you
as if your grave were already made."[6]

But in spite of Herrero Grande's warning and General
Carleton's continuous pursuit, Manuelito managed to avoid
capture all through the spring and summer of 1865. Freedom, even with so much danger, was better than a life of
imprisonment.

Late in the summer, Barboncito and several of his warriors
escaped from the Bosque Redondo; they were said to be far
away in Apache country. So many Navahos were leaving the
reservation now that General Carleton posted permanent
guards for forty miles around. In August the general ordered
the post commander to kill every Navaho found off the reservation without a pass.

When the Bosque's grain crops failed in the autumn of
1865, the Army gave the Navahos meal, flour, and bacon

which had been condemned as unfit for soldiers to eat. Deaths began to rise again; so did the number of attempted escapes.

Although General Carleton was being criticized now by New Mexicans for conditions at the Bosque Redondo, he continued to hunt down Navahos. At last, on September 1, 1866, the chief he wanted most—Manuelito—limped into Fort Wingate with twenty-three beaten warriors and surrendered. They were thin and hungry, dressed in rags. One of Manuelito's arms hung useless at his side from a wound. A short time later Barboncito came in with twenty-one followers and surrendered for the second time. Now there were no more war chiefs.

Ironically, only eighteen days after Manuelito surrendered, General Carleton was removed from command of the Army's Department of New Mexico. The Civil War, which had brought Star Chief Carleton to power, had been over for more than a year now, and the New Mexicans no longer wanted him in their territory.

When Manuelito arrived at the Bosque, a new superintendent was there, A. B. Norton. The superintendent examined the soil on the reservation and said no grain could be grown on it; he examined the water and said it was unhealthy. The reservation, Norton added, had cost the government millions of dollars.

> The sooner it is abandoned and the Indians removed, the better. . . . Do you expect an Indian to be satisfied and contented deprived of the common comforts of life, without which a white man would not be contented anywhere? . . . If they remain on this reservation they must always be held there by force, and not from choice. O! let them go back, or take them to where they can have good cool water to drink, wood plenty to keep them from freezing to death, and where the soil will produce something for them to eat.[7]

For two years officials from Washington came through the reservation to observe the conditions there. Some were truly sympathetic to the Navahos; some were mainly concerned with cutting down the costs.

"We were there for a few years," Manuelito remembered. "Many of our people died from the climate. . . . People from Washington held a council with us. . . . We promised to obey the laws if we were permitted to get back to our own country."

Before they could leave, the chiefs had to sign a new treaty (June 1, 1868) which began: "From this day forward all war between the parties to this agreement shall forever cease."

The Navahos were eager to be off. Manuelito said:

> The nights and days were long before it came time for us to go to our homes. The day before we were to start we went a little way towards home, because we were so anxious to start. We came back and the Americans gave us a little stock and we thanked them for that. We told the drivers to whip the mules, we were in such a hurry. When we saw the top of the mountain from Albuquerque we wondered if it was our mountain, and we felt like talking to the ground, we loved it so, and some of the old men and women cried with joy when they reached their homes.[8]

And so the Navahos returned to the land they had been so painfully torn away from. When the new reservation lines were made, much of their best pastureland was taken away for the white settlers. Life would not be easy. They would have to struggle to endure. But bad as it was, the Navahos would come to know that they were among the more fortunate of the western Indians. For the others, the ordeal had just begun.

2
Cochise and the Apache Guerrillas

When I was young I walked all over this country, east and west, and saw no other people than the Apaches. After many summers I walked again and found another race of people had come to take it. How is it? Why is it that the Apaches wait to die—that they carry their lives on their fingernails? They roam over the hills and plains and want the heavens to fall on them. The Apaches were once a great nation; they are now but few, and because of this they want to die and so carry their lives on their fingernails.

— COCHISE OF THE CHIRICAHUA APACHES

DURING GENERAL CARLETON'S SIEGE against the Indians of the Southwest, only one band of Apaches had been forced into imprisonment at the Bosque Redondo. These were the Mescalero Apaches who numbered less than a thousand. The majority of the tribe still roamed free.

Unlike their relatives the Navahos, the Apaches had never adjusted their way of life to the Spanish white man's. Instead of farming their land, they had defended it. In fighting against the Spaniards, the Apaches had learned how to torture and mutilate their victims. For generations they had fought a guerrilla war—few men against many, hiding, then attacking suddenly from the mountains. Because of their dar-

19

ing, the Apaches were well known and even feared by the Americans.

Cochise was the most famous Apache of them all. His band was the Chiricahuas. Cochise was taller than most Apaches, with broad shoulders and a large chest. His face was intelligent. White men who had met him said he had gentle manners and a neat, clean appearance.

When the Americans first came to Arizona, Cochise had welcomed them. He promised the military authorities that he would allow United States citizens to pass freely through Chiricahua country on the southern route to California. Even when the Overland Mail put a stage station in Apache Pass, Cochise did not object. Perhaps he could yet get along with these English-speaking white people.

Then, one day in February 1861, Cochise got a message from Apache Pass asking him to come to the station for a meeting with Lieutenant George Bascom, a military officer. Expecting nothing serious, Cochise took along five members of his family—a woman, a child, and three men. As soon as they entered Bascom's tent, soldiers surrounded it. The lieutenant accused the Chiricahuas of stealing some cattle and a half-breed boy from a ranch nearby.

Cochise had heard about the captured boy. A band of Coyotero Apaches had made the raid, he said; perhaps he would be able to arrange a ransom. In reply, Bascom ordered the arrest of Cochise and his relatives; they would be held as hostages until the cattle and the boy were returned.

At the moment the soldiers moved in to make the arrest, Cochise slashed a hole in the tent and fled. Because his relatives were still held as prisoners, Cochise and some warriors captured three white men and tried to make an exchange with the lieutenant. Bascom would not agree to the exchange unless the stolen cattle and the boy were included in it.

3. *Cochise. Reproduced from a painting in the Arizona Pioneers'*
Historical Society Library.

Angry because Bascom would not believe his people innocent, Cochise blocked Apache Pass and attacked the soldiers
at the stage station. After giving Bascom one more chance to
exchange, Cochise killed his prisoners, mutilating them with
lances, a cruel practice the Apaches had learned from the
Spaniards. A few days later Lieutenant Bascom retaliated by
hanging Cochise's three male relatives.

It was at this time that the Chiricahuas transferred their
hatred of the Spaniards to the Americans. For a quarter of a
century they and other Apaches would fight a guerrilla battle that would take more lives than any other Indian war.

At the time (1861) the greatest war chief of the Apaches
was Mangas Colorado, a seventy-year-old Mimbreño who
was even taller than the towering Cochise. Mangas had followers among many of the bands in southeastern Arizona and
southwestern New Mexico. Cochise was married to Mangas'
daughter. After Cochise's relatives were murdered, the two
men united to drive the Americans from their homeland.
They attacked wagon trains, stopped stagecoaches and mails,
and drove several hundred white miners out of their territory.
After the Bluecoats and the Graycoats began their Civil War,
Mangas and Cochise fought the Graycoats until they fled to
the east.

And then, in 1862, Star Chief Carleton came marching
from California with his thousands of Bluecoats, using the
old trail that ran through the heart of Chiricahua country.
They came in small groups at first, always stopping for water
at a spring near the abandoned stage station at Apache Pass.
But on July 15, in the Moon of the Horse, over three hundred
soldiers were sighted. Mangas and Cochise were waiting for
them along rocky heights overlooking the pass and spring.
Five hundred warriors attacked suddenly with bows and arrows. The soldiers retreated but when they came back it was

with wagons that had powerful guns inside. Suddenly great flashes of fire burst through Apache Pass. Clouds of black smoke filled the sky and a great thundering echoed among the high rocks. The Apaches had heard the little cannons of the Spaniards before. But these thundering wagon-guns made terror and death.

Still the Indians fought on, trying to regain their pass, with its sweet-flowing spring water. The following day Mangas was badly wounded. The Apache warriors broke off the fight and carried his bleeding body away.

Cochise was determined to save Mangas' life. Instead of trusting to the medicine men and their chants and rattles, he brought his father-in-law a hundred miles into Mexico to a famous surgeon. As he was presented with the helpless body of Mangas Colorado, the man was told: *Make him well. If he dies, this town will die.*

Some months later Mangas was back in his Mimbres Mountains wearing a broad-brimmed straw hat and a serape from Mexico. He was thinner and more wrinkled than before, but he could still outride and outshoot warriors half his age. While he was resting in his mountains, Mangas learned that the Bluecoats were killing Apaches everywhere with their wagon-guns, as they had killed his and Cochise's warriors at Apache Pass.

Mangas knew now that even his bravest young warriors could not defeat the great power of the United States. He had been wondering how to get peace for all the Apaches before he died. Mangas remembered the treaty he had signed at Santa Fe in 1852. In that year, the Apaches and the people of the United States had agreed to peace and friendship. But now there was only hostility and death. Perhaps it was time to make a new treaty with the Americans and their Bluecoat soldiers.

One day in January 1863, a Mexican came to Mangas'
camp under a truce flag. He said that some soldiers were
nearby and wanted to talk peace. The Mimbreños warriors
warned Mangas not to go. Did he not remember what happened to Cochise when he went to see Lieutenant Bascom at
Apache Pass? Mangas shrugged off their fears. After all he
was but an old man. What harm could the soldiers do to an
old man who only wanted to talk peace? He even refused
to let his warriors come with him. He was protected by a
truce, he told them, and would be perfectly safe. But as soon
as he reached the soldiers' camp, a dozen men with rifles
came out of the underbrush. Mangas was a prisoner.

Daniel Connor, a white miner who was present, observed
that, "the old chief . . . towered above everybody about him
in stature. He looked careworn and refused to talk and evidently felt that he had made a great mistake in trusting the
paleface on this occasion."[1]

That night Connor saw the two soldiers who were guarding
Mangas torturing him with bayonets that had been heated
in the fire. At last it seemed that the old chief could endure
it no longer. He began "telling the sentinels in Spanish that
he was no child to be playing with. But . . . he had hardly
begun his exclamations when both sentinels promptly brought
down their minié muskets to bear on him and fired, nearly
at the same time, through his body."

When Mangas fell back, the guards emptied their pistols
into his body. A soldier took his scalp, another cut off his
head and boiled the flesh away so he could sell the skull.
They dumped the headless body in a ditch. The official military report stated that Mangas was killed trying to escape.

After that, as Daniel Connor put it, "the Indians went to
war in earnest . . . they seemed bent on avenging his death
with all their power."[2]

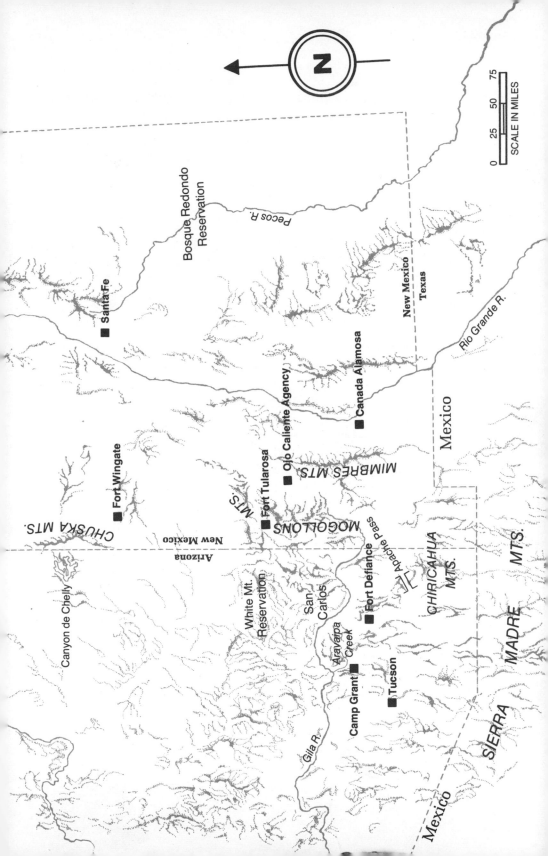

From the Chiricahua country of Arizona to the Mimbres Mountains of New Mexico, Cochise and his three hundred warriors began a campaign to drive out the white men or lose their lives in the attempt. Other Apache bands were fighting in their own territories. For years small armies of warriors kept the Southwest in turmoil. Although they generally stayed clear of American forts and settlements, whenever a rancher or miner got careless, a band of raiders would swoop down to capture horses or cattle.

When the Civil War ended and General Carleton left New Mexico, the United States government tried once to make peace with the Apaches. But since the terms were the usual ones—a life of imprisonment at the Bosque Redondo or other reservations—few Apaches would come in.

By 1870 raids were more frequent, and because Cochise was the best-known chief, he was usually blamed, no matter where they occurred.

That was why in the spring of 1871 the Commissioner of Indian Affairs in Washington invited Cochise for a meeting to help him bring about a permanent peace in Apache country. Cochise did not believe anything had changed. He still did not feel that he could trust any representative of the United States government. A few weeks later, after what happened to Eskiminzin and his band of Aravaipa Apaches, Cochise was even more positive that no Indian should ever again put his life in the hands of the treacherous Americans.

Eskiminzin and his hundred and fifty followers lived north of Cochise's stronghold along Aravaipa Creek, from which they took their name. One day in February 1871, Eskiminzin walked into Camp Grant, a small military post nearby, and asked to see the *capitán*, Lieutenant Royal Whitman.

Eskiminzin told Whitman that his people no longer had a

home and could not make one. The Bluecoats were always chasing them and shooting at them just because they were Apaches. He wanted to make peace so they could settle down and plant their crops by the Aravaipa as they and their fathers before them had always done.

Lieutenant Whitman was sympathetic. He agreed to let Eskiminzin's band stay near the fort as technical prisoners of war if they agreed to turn in their guns. The Aravaipas were happy to; some even turned in their bows and arrows as well. They established a village a few miles up the creek, planted corn, and began cooking mescal, their principal type of food. Impressed by their hard work, Whitman employed them to cut hay so they could earn money to buy supplies. Neighboring ranchers also took some of them as laborers.

Whitman meanwhile had written about the situation to his military superiors, asking for instructions. He did not hear from them immediately. Uneasy because all responsibility for Eskiminzin's Aravaipas was his, the lieutenant kept a close watch on their movements.

In April there were raids near Tucson and four white men were killed. Many of the citizens of that city were hoping to make money on a continuing Indian war. They did not like posts where Apaches worked and were peaceful. Eskiminzin's Aravaipas were therefore blamed for the murders even though their village was fifty-five miles away and it was unlikely they would have traveled so far to raid. On April 28, a hundred and forty well-armed vigilantes rode out from Tucson to attack the unarmed Aravaipas.

As soon as Lieutenant Whitman learned about the raid he took action. "I immediately sent the two interpreters, mounted, to the Indian camp," he later reported, "with orders to tell the chiefs the exact state of things, and for them to bring their entire party inside the post. . . . My messengers returned in about an hour, with intelligence that they could find no living Indians."[3]

When Whitman reached the village it was still burning, and the ground was covered with dead and mutilated bodies. "I found quite a number of women shot while asleep beside their bundles of hay which they had collected to bring in that morning. The wounded who were unable to get away had their brains beaten out with clubs or stones, while some were shot full of arrows after having been mortally wounded by gunshot. The bodies were all stripped . . . of the whole number buried [about a hundred] one was an old man and one was a well-grown boy—all the rest were women and children."

Whitman's persistent efforts finally brought the Tucson killers to trial. Their lawyers claimed that the citizens of Tucson had followed the trail of murdering Apaches straight to the Aravaipa village—even though four white men from Camp Grant all said that the Indians there had never made up a raiding party. The trial lasted for five days; the verdict was to release the Tucson killers.

As for Lieutenant Whitman, his unpopular defense of Apaches led to three court martials on ridiculous charges and eventually destroyed his military career.

The Camp Grant massacre, however, focused national attention upon the Apaches. President Grant described the attack as "purely murder" and ordered the Army and the Indian Bureau to bring peace to the Southwest.

In June 1871, two men arrived who wanted to arrange meetings with the leading Apache chiefs, particularly Cochise. General George Crook took command of the Department of Arizona, and Vincent Colyer, a representative from the Indian Bureau, set out first to find Eskiminzin.

The Aravaipa chief came out of the mountains willingly. "The commissioner probably thought he would see a great *capitán*," Eskiminzin said to Colyer, "but he only sees a very poor man and not very much of a *capitán* . . . three moons ago . . . I had many people, but many have been massacred. Now I have got few people . . . after that massacre who could have stood it? When I made peace with Lieutenant Whitman my heart was very big and happy. The people of Tucson . . . must be crazy. They acted as though they had neither heads nor hearts . . . they must have a thirst for our blood."[4]

Colyer expressed sympathy with the Aravaipas and promised to do what he could to help them. After finding Eskiminzin so ready to talk, he was encouraged about the possibility of arranging a meeting with Cochise.

General Crook was also searching throughout Arizona for the famous Apache leader. He ordered his soldiers to scour the Chiricahua Mountains to find him dead or alive. Gray Wolf was the name the Apaches gave General Crook. Cochise escaped Gray Wolf by crossing into New Mexico. He then sent a message to the Star Chief at Santa Fe, General Gordon Granger, stating that he would meet him to talk peace.

The place chosen was Cañada Alamosa, an agency or central administration point which had been set up by the Indian Bureau in New Mexico. When Granger arrived, Cochise was waiting for him. Both men were eager to get the matter settled. For Granger it was a chance to win fame as the man who took the surrender of the great Cochise. For Cochise it was the end of the road; he was almost sixty years old and was very tired; gray streaked his shoulder-length hair.

Granger explained that peace was possible only if the Chiricahuas agreed to live on a reservation. But Cochise ignored his specific remarks and replied in a quiet voice, seldom gesturing: "The sun has been very hot on my head and made me as in a fire; my blood was on fire, but now I have come into this valley and drunk of these waters and washed myself in them and they have cooled me. Now that I am cool I have come with my hands open to you to live in peace with you. I speak straight and do not wish to deceive or be deceived. I want a good, strong, and lasting peace."

When the discussion came around to a location for the Chiricahua reservation, Granger said the government wanted to move the agency from Cañada Alamosa to Fort Tularosa in the Mogollons.

"I want to live in these mountains," Cochise protested. "I do not want to go to Tularosa. That is a long ways off. The flies on those mountains eat out the eyes of the horses. The bad spirits live there. I have drunk of these waters and they have cooled me; I do not want to leave here."[5]

Cochise promised Granger to keep his people at peace, and the Chiricahuas were allowed to stay at Cañada Alamosa with its streams of clear water. Even though everything was going well, a few months later the government ordered all Apaches moved to Fort Tularosa. When Cochise heard the news, he slipped away with his warriors. They divided into small groups, fleeing once again to their dry and rocky Chiricahua Mountains in southeastern Arizona. This time, Cochise decided, he would stay there. Even the Gray Wolf, General Crook, could come after him; Cochise would fight him with rocks if need be.

In the Time When the Corn Is Taken In (September 1872) Cochise received reports from his lookouts that some white men were coming to his stronghold. One of them was Taglito—Tom Jeffords. Cochise had not seen Taglito for a long time.

Back in the old days, after Cochise and Mangas had gone

to war with the Bluecoats, Tom Jeffords used to carry the mail through Chiricahua territory. Apache warriors so often ambushed Jeffords that he almost gave up the job. Then one day he came all alone to Cochise's camp. He took off his weapons and walked over to where Cochise was sitting, with no show of fear. Taglito Jeffords told Cochise that he wanted a personal treaty so that he could carry the mail in peace. Cochise could do nothing but honor his courage. Jeffords was never ambushed again on his mail route. Many times afterward the tall red-bearded man came back to Cochise's camp and they would talk and drink tiswin beer together.

Cochise knew that if Taglito was with the white men coming into the mountains, they were searching for him. He waited until he was certain that everything was all right. Then he rode down to greet them. He got off his horse and embraced Taglito, who said in English to a white-bearded man in dusty clothing: "This is Cochise." The right sleeve of the bearded man's coat was empty; he looked like an old war veteran. He was General Oliver Otis Howard. *"Buenos días, señor,"* Cochise said, and they shook hands.

General Howard explained that he had been sent by President Grant to make peace. Cochise assured him that peace was what he wanted too. But the Chiricahuas could not live in imprisonment. "Why shut me up on a reservation?" he asked. "We will make peace. We will keep it faithfully. But let us go around free as Americans do. Let us go wherever we please." If there had to be boundaries, Cochise asked that they be put around Apache Pass in the Chiricahua Mountains.

General Howard was able to listen to Cochise better than any military official before him. He stayed in the Apache camp for eleven days and was completely won over by the courtesy and direct simplicity of Cochise. He was charmed by the Chiricahua women and children.

He wrote afterward, "I was forced . . . to give them, as

Cochise had suggested, a reservation embracing a part of the Chiricahua Mountains and of the valley adjoining on the west. . . ."[6]

One more matter had to be settled. By law a white man must be appointed agent for the new reservation. For Cochise this was no problem; there was only one white man that all the Chiricahuas trusted—Taglito, the red-bearded Tom Jeffords.

Eskiminzin's Aravaipa Apaches were less fortunate. After Commissioner Colyer's visit in 1871, the Aravaipas began to put their lives back together at Camp Grant. They rebuilt their village and replanted their grain fields. Just as everything seemed to be going well, however, the government decided to move Camp Grant and clear the area of Indians.

In February 1873, the Aravaipas were transferred to San Carlos, a new Apache agency on the Gila River. Shortly afterward a white soldier chief was killed in an uprising there. Eskiminzin was arrested as a "military precaution" even though neither he nor any of the Aravaipas had anything to do with the killing.

He remained a prisoner until the night of January 4, 1874, when he escaped and led his people away from San Carlos. For four cold months the Aravaipas roamed through unfamiliar mountains in search of food and shelter. Finally, to keep them from dying, Eskiminzin went back to San Carlos. "We have done nothing wrong," he told the agent, "but we are afraid. That is why we ran away. Now we come back. If we stay in the mountains we will die of hunger and cold-sickness. If American soldiers kill us here, it will be just the same. We will not run away again."

As soon as the agent reported the Aravaipas' return, the Army sent an order to arrest Eskiminzin once more. He and

4. *Eskiminzin, head chief of the Aravaipa Apaches. Photographed probably by Charles M. Bell in Washington, D.C., 1876. Courtesy of the Smithsonian Institution.*

his subchiefs were taken to the new Camp Grant and kept chained together while they made adobe bricks. At night they slept in their chains on the ground and ate food discarded by the soldiers.

One day in the summer of 1874, a young white man came to see Eskiminzin. He was John Clum, the new agent at San Carlos. He said the Aravaipas needed their chief to lead them. "Why are you a prisoner?" Clum asked.

"I have done nothing," Eskiminzin replied. "White men tell lies about me, maybe. I always try to do right."[7]

John Clum said he would arrange his release if Eskiminzin would promise to help him improve conditions at San Carlos. Two months later the Aravaipa chief rejoined his people. Once again the future looked promising, but he was wise enough not to hope for too much. Since the coming of the white men, he had learned that the future for any Apache was very uncertain.

In the spring of 1874 Cochise became very ill. Tom Jeffords, now the Chiricahua agent, brought an army surgeon to examine his old friend, but the surgeon could not diagnose the ailment.

During this time the government decided that money could be saved by moving the Chiricahuas to a new reservation in New Mexico. When officials came to discuss the matter with Cochise he said the transfer made no difference to him. He would be dead before he could be moved. His subchiefs and his sons objected, however. They said if the agency was moved, they would not go. Not even the United States had enough soldiers to move them. They would rather die in the Chiricahua Mountains.

After the government officials left, Cochise became so weak and was suffering such pain that Jeffords decided to get the surgeon once more. As he was about to leave, Cochise asked, "Do you think you will see me alive again?"

Jeffords replied with the frankness of a brother: "No, I do not think I will."

"I think I will die about ten o'clock tomorrow morning. Do you think we will see each other again?"

Jeffords was silent for a moment. "I don't know. What do you think about it?"

"I don't know," Cochise answered. "It is not clear to my mind, but I think we will, somewhere up there."[8]

Cochise was dead before Jeffords returned with the surgeon. After a few days, the agent told the Chiricahuas that he felt it was time for him to leave. They would not hear of it. Cochise's sons, Taza and Naiche, were particularly insistent. If Taglito deserted them, they said, the promises made between Cochise and the government would be worthless. Jeffords promised to stay.

By the springtime of 1875 most of the Apache bands were either living on reservations or had fled into Mexico. In March the Army transferred General Crook to the Great Plains. The Sioux and the Cheyennes, who had endured reservation life longer than the Apaches, were becoming rebellious.

A forced peace lay over the deserts, peaks, and mesas of the Apache country. It would not last for long. The demands of local citizens for Indian land and the prejudice against Apaches as bloodthirsty savages would not be satisfied until every bit of dignity and freedom remaining to them had been taken away.

3

The Last of
the Apache Chiefs

*I was praying to the light and to the darkness, to God and to
the sun, to let me live quietly there with my family. I don't know
what the reason was that people should speak badly of me. Very
often there are stories put in the newspapers that I am to be
hanged. I don't want that anymore. When a man tries to do right,
such stories ought not to be put in the newspapers. There are
very few of my men left now. They have done some bad things
but I want them all rubbed out now and let us never speak of
them again. There are very few of us left.*

—GOYATHLAY (GERONIMO)

By 1875 the United States government's Indian policy was
to gather as many tribes as possible on large regional reservations. White Mountain, 2.5 million acres in eastern Arizona, was larger than all the other Apache reservations in the
Southwest combined. Its agency, San Carlos, was headed by
John Clum. Seven different Apache bands were administered
from here, including Eskiminzin's Aravaipas.

The agency was not a pleasant place. One army officer
wrote, "Rain was so infrequent that it took on the semblance
of a phenomenon when it came at all. Almost continuously
dry, hot, dust-and-gravel-laden winds swept the plain, de-
nuding it of every vestige of vegetation. In summer a temperature of 110° in the shade was cool weather. At all other

times of the year flies, gnats, unnamable bugs . . . swarmed in the millions."[1]

Yet John Clum had managed to keep peace at San Carlos. Unlike most reservations, the Indians there were allowed to make their own decisions. In his stubborn way, Clum had forced the military out of the vast White Mountain reservation. A company of Apaches was trained to police the agency. An Apache courts system was established to try offenders.

On May 3, 1876, agent Clum received orders from the Commissioner of Indian Affairs to go to Apache Pass and remove the Chiricahuas from the reservation that General Oliver Otis Howard had granted them three and a half years earlier.

Since Cochise's death in 1874, his oldest son, Taza, had become chief of the Chiricahuas. But he was not a strong leader. In spite of efforts by both Taza and Tom Jeffords— who continued to act as agent at Apache Pass—the raiding which Cochise had strictly forbidden started up again. Because the Chiricahua reservation was a stopping point for raiding parties going in and out of Arizona and Mexico, the United States government had decided to move the band to San Carlos.

John Clum doubted that the freedom-loving Chiricahuas would adjust to the regulated life on White Mountain reservation, but he had to carry out his orders. When he arrived at Apache Pass, he was surprised to find Taza and Tom Jeffords cooperative. Taza, like his father, wanted to keep peace. If the Chiricahuas must leave their homeland and go to White Mountain to keep the peace, they would do so. Only about half the Chiricahuas, however, followed Taza to San Carlos. The rest fled into Mexico. Among their leaders was a forty-six-year-old Apache who had first fought with Mangas Colorado, and then later with Cochise. He was Goyathlay, better known to the white men as Geronimo.

During the winter of 1876–77, Geronimo and his band made many raids upon their old enemies, the Mexicans, and accumulated large herds of cattle and horses. That spring Geronimo brought the stolen livestock up to New Mexico and sold them to white ranchers for guns, hats, boots, and much whiskey. These Chiricahuas settled down in a hideout near some Mimbreño cousins. The agency there was called Ojo Caliente—the Warm Springs.

In March 1877, John Clum received new orders from Washington. He was to take his Apache police to Ojo Caliente and transfer the Indians there to San Carlos. In addition, he was to arrest Geronimo and any other "renegade" Chiricahuas he could find.

Geronimo was captured and spent four months in prison before being released, but the Warm Springs Apaches with their chief, Victorio, were sent to San Carlos immediately. Clum tried to win Victorio's trust by giving him more authority than the chief had ever had at Ojo Caliente. For a short while it seemed as if peaceful Apache communities could be developed on the White Mountain reservation. Suddenly, the Army moved a company of soldiers in—a precaution, military officials said, because there were now so many rebellious Apaches at San Carlos.

John Clum was furious. He telegraphed the Commissioner of Indian Affairs asking if he could enlist more Apache police to replace the Army. He wanted the soldiers removed immediately; they would cause trouble among the Indians. Even though Clum had succeeded in keeping peace in the White Mountain reservation, the government refused to listen to his demands. John Clum resigned and the Army stayed.

Before summer's end of 1877, conditions at San Carlos became chaotic. Although there were hundreds more Indians

5. *Geronimo. From a photograph taken by A. Frank Randall in 1886.*
Courtesy of the Smithsonian Institution.

now, extra supplies came in slowly. To make matters worse, instead of giving out rations at various camps, the new agent made all the bands come to the main agency building. Some of the Apaches had to walk twenty miles. If old people and children could not come, they received no rations. Miners began to move onto the edges of the reservation and would not leave. The Apache police system established by Clum began to break down.

On the night of September 2, Victorio led his band off the reservation and started back to Ojo Caliente. Apache police followed them, recaptured the horses they had taken from the reservation corrals, then let the people go. They were allowed to stay at Ojo Caliente for a year until late in 1878, when orders came to take them back to San Carlos. Victorio escaped from the soldiers, but eventually agreed to live at Fort Tularosa. Just as these Apaches began life over again for the third time in two years, some lawmen came to arrest Victorio on an old charge of horse stealing and murder. He ran away and resolved never again to put himself at the mercy of white people by living on a reservation. He was convinced that he had been marked for death and that all Apaches were doomed unless they fought back as they had been doing in Mexico since the coming of the Spaniards.

Establishing a stronghold in Mexico, Victorio began gathering a guerrilla army "to make war forever" on the United States. Before the end of 1879 he had a warrior band of two hundred Mescaleros, Chiricahuas, and Mimbreños. To get horses and supplies, they raided Mexican ranches, then made daring trips into New Mexico and Texas, killing settlers where they could find them, ambushing pursuing soldiers, and then dashing back across the border.

As he fought battle after battle, Victorio's hatred deepened. He became a ruthless killer, torturing and mutilating his victims. Some of his followers considered him a madman and left him. A price of three thousand dollars was placed on his head. Finally on October 14, 1880, Mexican soldiers trapped Victorio's band. They slaughtered seventy-eight Apaches, including Victorio, and took the women and children as captives. Only thirty warriors escaped alive.

Among those who escaped was a Mimbreño warrior who had already passed his seventieth birthday. His name was Nana. He had been fighting Spanish-speaking white men and English-speaking white men for as long as he could remember. In Nana's mind there was no doubt that the resistance must continue. During the summer of 1881, Nana and a handful of followers crossed the Rio Grande, fought eight battles, and escaped back into Mexico with a thousand cavalrymen close behind. Although the raids were nowhere near White Mountain, the Army reacted by sending hundreds of soldiers to guard the reservation.

Rumors spread quickly among the Apache camps; it was said that the Army was planning to arrest all leaders who had ever been hostile. One night late in September, Geronimo and about seventy Chiricahuas slipped out of White Mountain and raced southward for their old Sierra Madre stronghold in Mexico.

Six months later, well armed and equipped, the Chiricahuas returned to White Mountain. They were determined to free all the Apaches who wanted to return to Mexico with them. It was a daring adventure. They galloped in and quickly organized the remaining Chiricahuas and Apaches from Ojo Caliente to leave for Mexico. But just after they crossed the border, they met a Mexican regiment that killed many men and most of the women and children who were riding in front.

Geronimo was one of the chiefs who escaped. Bitter, with most of his warriors dead, he joined up with old Nana and his guerrillas. For all of them, it was now a war of survival.

Each new outbreak at White Mountain had brought an increase in the number of soldiers. They swarmed everywhere. Each increase brought more unrest among the Apaches on the reservation, more flights to Mexico, and more raiding against ranchers along the escape routes.

The Army again called on General George Crook—now quite a different man from the one who had left Arizona ten years earlier to go north to fight the Sioux and Cheyennes. His experiences had shown him that Indians were human beings—a viewpoint that most of his fellow officers had not yet accepted.

In September 1882, Crook arrived at the White Mountain reservation. Instead of listening to the military officers, he searched out individual Apaches and listened to their stories. "They told me . . . that they had lost confidence in everybody, and did not know whom or what to believe; that they were constantly told, by irresponsible parties, that they were to be disarmed, that they were to be attacked by troops on the reservation, and removed from their country; and that they were fast arriving at the conclusion that it would be more manly to die fighting than to be thus destroyed."

Early in his investigations, Crook did in fact discover that white men were trying to trick the Apaches and make them commit violent actions. In this way, they could be driven from the reservation, leaving it open for land-grabbing.[2]

Crook ordered the removal of all white squatters and miners from the reservation and then demanded complete cooperation from the Indian Bureau in starting reforms. Instead of having to live near San Carlos, the different bands could build their homes and ranches on any part of the reservation they chose. The Army would buy farm produce from the

6. *Victorio. Courtesy of Arizona Pioneers' Historical Society Library.*

Indians rather than from white suppliers. The Indians would be expected to govern themselves, to reorganize their police and hold their courts, as they had done under John Clum. Crook promised that no soldiers would come on their reservation provided they could control themselves.

The Apaches were skeptical. They remembered Crook's harsh ways in the old days when he was the Gray Wolf hunting down Cochise and the Chiricahuas, but they soon discovered that he meant what he said. Once more there were enough rations and no soldiers bullied them. They were free again, as long as they stayed inside the reservation.

But they could not forget their relatives who were truly free in Mexico. There were always a few young men slipping southward and returning with exciting news of adventures and good times.

Crook also gave much thought to Geronimo and the Apaches who were fugitives in Mexico. There was great pressure from the white settlers in Arizona and New Mexico to go to war against them. The situation had been created largely by lurid newspaper tales. As Crook said:

> border newspapers . . . disseminate all sorts of exaggerations and falsehoods about the Indians . . . while the Indians' side of the case is rarely heard. In this way the people at large get false ideas with reference to the matter. Then when the outbreak does come public attention is turned to the Indians, their crimes and atrocities are alone condemned, while the persons whose injustice has driven them to this course escape scot free. . . . No one knows this fact better than the Indian, therefore he is excusable in seeing no justice in a government which only punishes him, while it allows the white man to plunder him as he pleases.[3]

Crook believed that he could convince Geronimo and the other guerrilla leaders of his good intentions—not by fighting them but by talking with them. The best place for this would be in one of their own Mexican strongholds away from rumor-spreading newspapers trying to stir up a profit-making, land-grabbing war.

The United States government had recently signed an agreement with the Mexican government permitting soldiers of each country to cross the border to find hostile Apaches. In March 1883, a mining camp near Tombstone, Arizona, was raided. It was the excuse Crook had been waiting for to enter Mexico. Several weeks later he found the Chiricahuas' camp, and in May he was able to capture the women and children while Geronimo was away leading a raid against Mexican ranchers.

The Apache chief had no choice but to surrender. After three long talks he and Crook at last came to an agreement. Geronimo said that he had always wanted peace but had been ill-treated at San Carlos by bad white men. Crook agreed that this was probably true, but if Geronimo wanted to return to the reservation he would be treated fairly. All Chiricahuas who returned, however, would have to work at farming and stock raising to make their own livings. "I am not taking your arms from you," Crook added, "because I am not afraid of you."[4]

Geronimo liked Crook's blunt manner, but he decided to test him to make certain the general truly trusted him. "I will remain here," he said, "until I have gathered up the last man, woman, and child of the Chiricahuas."[5] To Geronimo's surprise, Crook agreed to the proposition.

Eight months passed, and then it was Crook's turn to be surprised. True to his word, Geronimo crossed the border in February 1884, and was taken to San Carlos.

For more than a year, General Crook could boast that "not an outrage or depredation of any kind" was committed by the Indians of Arizona and New Mexico. Geronimo and the other Chiricahua leaders competed to develop their *ranchos*, and Crook made sure that their agent issued enough supplies. Many white people, however, thought Crook had been too easy on the Apaches; the newspapers he had criticized for writing falsely about the Indians now turned on him. Some even claimed that Crook had surrendered to Geronimo in Mexico and had made a deal with the Chiricahua chief in order to escape alive. As for Geronimo, they made a special villain of him, inventing many stories of his cruelty and calling on vigilantes to hang him if the government would not.

After the Corn Planting Time (spring of 1885) the Chiricahuas grew discontented. There was little for the men to do except sit around, gamble, quarrel, and drink tiswin beer. Tiswin was forbidden on the reservation; but the Chiricahuas had plenty of corn for brewing it, and drinking was one of the few pleasures of the old days left to them.

On the night of May 17, Geronimo, old Nana, and some other Chiricahua leaders got drunk on tiswin and decided to go to Mexico. With them were ninety-two women and children, eight youths, and thirty-four men. As they left San Carlos, Geronimo cut the telegraph wires.

Many reasons were given for this sudden flight when everything had seemed to be going smoothly. Some said it was because of the tiswin spree; others said that the bad stories the newspapers had printed about the Chiricahuas made them fear being arrested and even hung.

The flight of Geronimo's band across Arizona was the signal for an outpouring of wild rumors. Newspapers featured big headlines: THE APACHES ARE OUT! The very word "Geronimo" became a cry for blood. General Crook was called upon to rush soldiers to protect defenseless white citizens from murderous Apaches. Geronimo, however, was

7. *Nana. Courtesy of Arizona Pioneers' Historical Society Library.*

desperately trying to escape confrontations with white citizens; all he wanted was to speed his people across the border to the old Sierra Madre sanctuary. For two days and nights the Chiricahuas rode without making camp.

Crook meanwhile was trying to avoid the vast military attack that public opinion was demanding of him. He knew that personal negotiation was the only way to deal with three dozen Apache warriors. As autumn approached, it became evident that he would have to cross the border into Mexico once again. His orders from Washington were clear: kill the fugitives or take their unconditional surrenders.

By this time the Chiricahuas had discovered that the Mexican Army was waiting for them in the Sierra Madre Mountains. Since the Mexicans wanted only to kill them whereas the Americans were willing to make prisoners of them, Geronimo and the other leaders finally decided to meet with Crook.

On March 25, 1886, the "hostile" Apache chiefs came in to surrender a few miles south of the border. "I give myself up to you," Geronimo said. "Do with me what you please. I surrender. Once I moved about like the wind. Now I surrender to you and that is all."[6] When Geronimo learned that he would be taken to the East, to Florida, as a prisoner, he asked that after two years he be allowed to return to the reservation. Crook thought the proposition over; it seemed fair to him. Believing that he could convince Washington that such a surrender was better than no surrender, he agreed.

Crook left the Chiricahuas to telegraph the War Department in Washington the new terms he had given for surrender. But while he was away, a white trader filled the Apaches with whiskey and lies about how the citizens of Arizona would hang them if they returned. Geronimo bolted, taking some thirty followers with him. "I feared treachery," he said afterward, "and when we became suspicious, we turned back."[7]

As a result of Geronimo's flight, the War Department severely criticized Crook for his carelessness, for granting unauthorized surrender terms, and for his tolerant attitude toward Indians. He immediately resigned and was replaced by Nelson Miles, whom the Indians called Bear Coat.

Bear Coat Miles took command on April 12, 1886. He quickly put five thousand soldiers into the field. He had, in addition, five hundred Apache scouts and thousands of civilian militia. The enemy to be conquered by this powerful military force was Geronimo and his "army" of twenty-four warriors, who were also pursued by thousands of Mexican soldiers throughout the summer of 1886.

When Geronimo was finally tracked down in a canyon of the Sierra Madres, he calmly laid down his rifle and asked the American officer in command how the Chiricahuas were getting along back in the United States. He then wanted to know all about Bear Coat Miles: Was his voice harsh or agreeable? Was he cruel or kind-hearted? Did he look you in the eyes or down at the ground when he talked? Would he keep his promises? Then he said to the officer: "We want your advice. Consider yourself one of us and not a white man. Remember all that has been said today, and as an Apache, what would you advise us to do under the circumstances?"

"I would trust General Miles and take him at his word," the officer replied.[8]

And so Geronimo surrendered for the last time. The Great Father in Washington (Grover Cleveland), who believed all the newspaper tales of Geronimo's evil deeds, recommended that he be hanged. The advice of men who knew better won out, and Geronimo and his surviving warriors were shipped as prisoners to Florida. He found most of his friends dying in the warm and humid land so unlike the high, dry country of their birth. The government had taken all their children away from them and sent them to an Indian school far away in Pennsylvania where they died too. The Chiricahuas were marked for extinction.

But they were not alone. Eskiminzin of the Aravaipas, who had become economically independent on the ranch he had developed near San Carlos, was arrested on the charge of communicating with an outlaw known as the Apache kid. He and the forty surviving Aravaipas were sent to live first in Florida, then in Alabama.

At last, a few friends such as George Crook and John Clum succeeded in having the Apaches sent back to the Southwest before they all died from a disease diagnosed as consumption. Eskiminzin and the Aravaipas returned to San Carlos. But the citizens of Arizona refused to admit Geronimo's Chiricahuas back in the state. When the Kiowas and Comanches learned of the Chiricahuas' plight, they offered their old Apache enemies a part of their reservation in Oklahoma. In 1894, Geronimo brought the surviving exiles to Fort Sill. When he died there in 1909, still a prisoner of war, he was buried in the Apache cemetery. A legend persists that not long afterward his bones were secretly removed to the Southwest—perhaps to the Mogollons, or the Chiricahua Mountains, perhaps to the Sierra Madre Mountains of Mexico. He was the last of the Apache chiefs.

Part Two

THE CHEYENNES
AND
THE SIOUX:

TRIBES OF THE GREAT PLAINS

4

War Comes to the Cheyennes

*Although wrongs have been done me I live in hopes. I have
not got two hearts. . . . Now we are together again to make
peace. My shame is as big as the earth, although I will
do what my friends advise me to do. I once thought that
I was the only man that persevered to be the friend of the
white man, but since they have come and cleaned out our lodges,
horses, and everything else, it is hard for me to believe white
men anymore.*
   —MOTAVATO (BLACK KETTLE) OF THE SOUTHERN CHEYENNES

THE CHEYENNES were one of the larger tribes of Plains Indians. In the old days, before white settlers came, the Cheyennes had lived in the woodlands of Minnesota. Gradually
they moved westward and acquired horses. Now the tribe
was geographically divided. The Northern Cheyennes shared
the Powder River country with the Sioux, frequently camping near them. The Southern Cheyennes had drifted below
the Platte River, establishing villages on the Colorado and
Kansas plains.

The Arapahos were old associates of the Cheyennes and
lived in the same areas. Some remained with the Northern
Cheyennes, others followed the Southern branch.

Together, these tribes ranged across a vast expanse of

territory. They were determined not to surrender it. In 1851, when United States officials asked if they could build roads and military posts across Cheyenne and Arapaho lands, the Indians consented. However the treaty they signed at Fort Laramie at that time clearly stated that they would continue to hold all rights or claims to the lands.

By the end of the first decade following the treaty signing, white men were everywhere. During the Pike's Peak gold rush of 1858, miners by the thousands came to dig yellow metal out of the Indians' earth. The miners built little wooden villages, and in 1859 they built a big village which they called Denver City. The Platte Valley, which had once teemed with buffalo, began to fill with settlers staking out ranches and land claims on territory the Laramie treaty had assigned to Southern Cheyennes and Arapahos.

After the Territory of Colorado was created by Congress in 1861, United States officials invited the Indian leaders to another meeting. They wanted to get a new treaty that would grant legal rights to the land American citizens had already taken. But because only six of the forty-four Cheyenne chiefs were present to sign the document, its legality was to remain in doubt.

During the first years of the white man's Civil War, Cheyenne and Arapaho hunting parties found it difficult to stay clear of Bluecoat soldiers who were scouting southward in search of Graycoats. Because the chiefs knew and feared the fate of the eastern tribes and of the Navahos, they tried to keep their young men busy hunting buffalo, away from the white men's routes of travel. But by the spring of 1864, soldiers were prowling into remote hunting grounds between the Smoky Hill and Republican rivers.

When the grass was well up that year, Roman Nose and quite a number of the Dog Soldier Cheyennes went north

8. *Roman Nose, of the Southern Cheyennes. Either photographed or copied by A. Zeno Shindler in Washington, D.C., 1868. Courtesy of the Smithsonian Institution.*

to the Powder River country for better hunting with their Northern Cheyenne cousins. Black Kettle, White Antelope, and Lean Bear kept their bands below the Platte, but were careful to avoid soldiers and white buffalo hunters by staying away from forts and settlements.

In the middle of May, Black Kettle and Lean Bear heard that soldiers had attacked some Cheyennes on the South Platte River. They decided to break camp and move northward to join the rest of the tribe for strength and protection.

Only the year before the two chiefs had been invited to visit the Great Father, Abraham Lincoln, in Washington. President Lincoln gave them medals to wear, and Colonel A. B. Greenwood, Commissioner of Indian Affairs, gave Black Kettle a United States flag with white stars for the thirty-four states bigger than glittering stars in the sky on a clear night. Colonel Greenwood had told him that as long as that flag flew above him no soldiers would ever fire upon him. Black Kettle was very proud of his flag and always mounted it on a pole above his tepee.

On the morning after the two chiefs set out on their journey, some hunters came hurrying back to camp. They had seen soldiers with cannons coming. Lean Bear liked excitement, and he told Black Kettle he would meet the soldiers and find out what they wanted. He hung the medal from the Great Father Lincoln outside his coat and took some papers he had been given in Washington certifying that he was a good friend of the United States.

Wolf Chief, one of the young warriors who went with Lean Bear, said afterward that the soldiers formed a line as soon as they saw the Cheyennes.

> Lean Bear told us warriors to stay where we were so as not
> to frighten the soldiers, while he rode forward to shake
> hands with the officer and show his papers. . . . When the

chief was within only twenty or thirty yards of the line, the officer called out in a very loud voice and the soldiers all opened fire on Lean Bear and the rest of us. Lean Bear fell off his horse right in front of the troops, and Star, another Cheyenne, also fell off his horse. The soldiers then rode forward and shot Lean Bear and Star again as they lay helpless on the ground.[1]

Black Kettle could not understand why the soldiers had attacked a peaceful Cheyenne camp without warning. He grieved for Lean Bear; they had been friends for almost half a century. At last Black Kettle decided what he must do. If anyone would know the reason for the killing it would be the Little White Man, William Bent. For over thirty years the Little White Man had lived on the Arkansas River. He was married to a Cheyenne woman and had five children who lived much of the time with their mother's people.

A week later Black Kettle met with William Bent. Both were concerned over the future of the Cheyennes. Bent knew of two more unprovoked attacks that had happened in other places. A soldier chief named John M. Chivington was responsible for the actions. His men had been given orders to "kill Cheyennes whenever and wherever found."[2] Among the Indians killed were two women and two children.

If such incidents continued, William Bent and Black Kettle agreed, a general war was bound to break out all over the plains. "It is not my intention or wish to fight the whites," Black Kettle said. "I want to be friendly and peaceable and keep my tribe so. I am not able to fight the whites. I want to live in peace."[3]

Bent told Black Kettle to keep his young men from making revenge raids and promised that he would try to persuade the military authorities to stop attacking Indians without cause. He then set out for Fort Lyon to speak with Colonel

Chivington, but the colonel claimed he was not authorized to make peace.

Late in June the governor of Colorado Territory, John Evans, sent out a circular addressed to the "friendly Indians of the plains," telling them that some members of their tribes had gone to war with the white people. He said nothing about soldiers attacking Indians, although this was the way all three fights with the Cheyennes had begun. "For this the Great Father is angry," he went on, "and will certainly hunt them out and punish them, but he does not want to injure those who remain friendly to the whites; he desires to protect and take care of them." Evans ordered friendly Cheyennes and Arapahos to report to Fort Lyon where they would be safe.[4]

As soon as William Bent learned of Governor Evans' decree he tried to warn the Indians to come in to Fort Lyon. Because the various bands were scattered across western Kansas for their summer hunts, several weeks passed before runners could reach all of them. During this period, clashes between soldiers and Indians steadily increased. William Bent's half-breed son George, who was with a large band of Cheyennes in July, said they were attacked again and again by the troops without any cause. They began retaliating in the only way they knew how—burning stage stations, chasing coaches, running off stock, and stopping wagon trains.

Black Kettle and the older chiefs tried to stop these raids, but their influence was weakened by the appeal of younger leaders such as Roman Nose and by members of the *Hotami-tanio,* or Dog Soldier Society.

At the end of August, Evans sent out a second proclamation "authorizing all citizens of Colorado . . . to go in pursuit of all hostile Indians on the plains, scrupulously avoiding those who have responded to my call to rendezvous

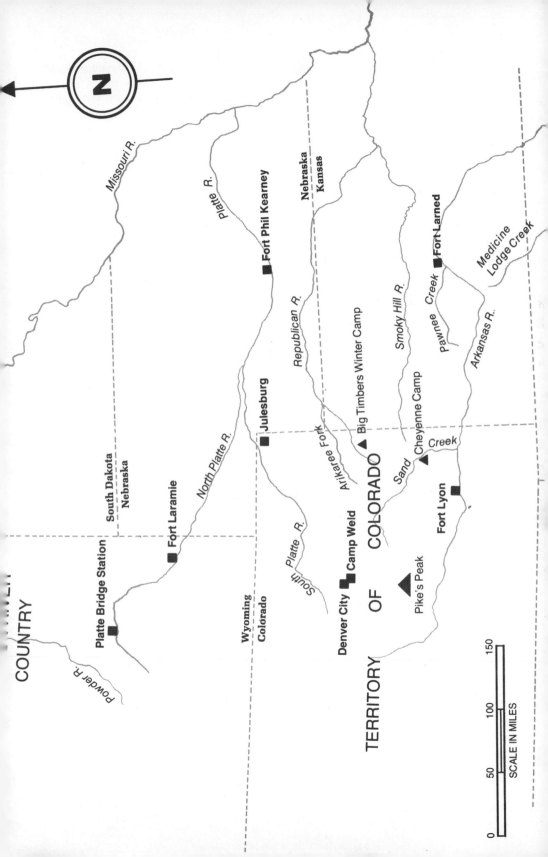

at the points indicated; also to kill and destroy as enemies of the country wherever they may be found, all such hostile Indians."[5]

By the time Black Kettle finally received Bent's message to come in to Fort Lyon, soldiers and bands of Governor Evans' armed citizens were searching Colorado for hostile Indians to attack. The six-day journey from their camps on the Smoky Hill would be too dangerous for the Cheyennes to make alone. Black Kettle sent two men, Eagle Head and One-Eye, ahead to Fort Lyon to ask for a military guide to take the band across Colorado. They carried a letter stating that the Cheyennes held seven white captives; four of them had been purchased from a raiding party with Black Kettle's own ponies.

The commanding officer at Fort Lyon, Major Edward W. Wynkoop, was immediately suspicious of the Indians' motives. When he learned from One-Eye that Black Kettle wanted his force of about a hundred soldiers to escort two thousand Cheyennes and Arapahos back to the post, he feared a trap. He decided finally to make the journey—not for the Indians' sake, but to rescue the white prisoners. It was probably for this reason that Black Kettle had mentioned the prisoners in his letter; he knew that no white man could stand the thought of white women and children living with Indians.

On September 6 Tall Chief Wynkoop and his soldiers were ready to march. Eagle Head and One-Eye would be both guides and hostages for the journey. "At the first sign of treachery from your people," Wynkoop warned them, "I will kill you."

"The Cheyennes do not break their word," One-Eye replied. "If they should do so, I would not care to live longer."

(Wynkoop said afterward that his conversations with the

two Cheyennes on this march made him change his long-held opinion of Indians. "I felt myself in the presence of superior beings; and these were the representatives of a race that I heretofore looked upon without exception as being cruel, treacherous, and bloodthirsty without feeling or affection for friend or kindred."[6])

After Tall Chief Wynkoop reached the Indians' camp, Black Kettle and the other chiefs met with him for a council. Some spoke angrily because so many Cheyennes and Arapahos had been killed without reason. But when Wynkoop promised that he would do everything that he could to stop the soldiers from fighting them, the Indians began to trust him. He said he was not a big chief, but if they would give him the white captives, he would go to Denver with the Indian leaders and help them make peace with the bigger chiefs.

The four captives that Black Kettle had ransomed were all children and seemed unharmed; in fact, when a soldier asked eight-year-old Ambrose Archer how the Indians had treated him, the boy replied that he "would just as lief stay with the Indians as not."[7]

Tall Chief Wynkoop's caravan of mounted soldiers, the four white children, and seven Indian leaders reached Denver on September 28. For the journey, Black Kettle mounted his big United States flag on the Indians' mule-drawn flatbed wagon. When they entered the dusty streets of Denver the Stars and Stripes fluttered protectively over the heads of the chiefs. All of Denver turned out for the procession.

Before the council began, Wynkoop went to see Governor Evans. The governor was reluctant to have anything to do with the Indians. He said the Cheyennes and Arapahos should be punished before giving them any peace. In any case, he had his soldiers to consider. "But what shall I do with the Third Colorado Regiment if I make peace?" Evans asked.

"They have been raised to kill Indians, and they must kill Indians." Eventually, however, Evans agreed to meet with Black Kettle and the other chiefs. After all, they had come four hundred miles to see him in response to his proclamation.[8]

The council was held at Camp Weld near Denver. Governor Evans brusquely asked the chiefs what they had to say. It was Black Kettle who spoke first:

> On sight of your circular of June 27, 1864, I took hold of the matter, and have now come to talk to you about it. . . . Major Wynkoop proposed that we come to see you. We have come with our eyes shut, following his handful of men, like coming through the fire. All we ask is that we may have peace with the whites. . . . The sky has been dark since the war began. . . . We want to take good tidings home to our people, that they may sleep in peace. I want you to give all these chiefs of the soldiers here to understand that we are for peace, and that we have made peace, that we may not be mistaken by them for enemies.

Throughout the council, Evans accused the Cheyenne and Arapaho chiefs of forming an alliance with the Sioux and taking part in raids along the Platte River. He barely listened to their denials. At last he called on Colonel Chivington, the man who had originally ordered the attacks against the Cheyennes. Chivington said merely that they should report to Major Wynkoop.[9]

And so the council ended, leaving the chiefs confused about whether they had made peace or not. They were sure of one thing—the only real friend they could count on among the soldiers was Tall Chief Wynkoop.

"So now we broke up our camp on the Smoky Hill and moved down to Sand Creek, about forty miles northeast of Fort Lyon," George Bent said. "From this new camp the

9. *Cheyenne and Arapaho chiefs meeting at the Camp Weld Council on September 28, 1864. Standing, third from left: John Smith, interpreter; to his left, White Wing and Bosse. Seated left to right: Neva, Bull Bear, Black Kettle, One-Eye, and an unidentified Indian. Kneeling left to right: Major Edward Wynkoop, Captain Silas Soule.*

Indians went in and visited Major Wynkoop, and the people at the fort seemed so friendly that after a short time the Arapahos left us and moved right down to the fort, where they went into camp and received regular rations."[10]

Wynkoop's humane treatment of the Indians soon brought him trouble with military officials in Colorado and Kansas. He was reprimanded for taking the chiefs to Denver without permission and was accused of "letting the Indians run things at Fort Lyon." On November 5, Major Scott J. Anthony, one of Chivington's officers, was sent to replace him as commander of the post.

As soon as Wynkoop left, Anthony began to lay plans for an all-out attack on the Cheyennes camped at Sand Creek. When a delegation of Indians, including Black Kettle, came to see the new soldier chief he pretended to be friendly. Several officers who were at the meeting said later that Anthony had assured the Cheyennes they would be under the protection of Fort Lyon if they returned to their camp at Sand Creek. He also told them that their young men could go east toward the Smoky Hill to hunt buffalo until he could issue winter rations.

Black Kettle was pleased. He and the other Cheyenne leaders had been thinking of moving far south of the Arkansas River so they would feel safe from the soldiers, but the words of Major Anthony made them feel safe at Sand Creek. They would stay there for the winter.

Immediately after the Cheyennes left, Anthony ordered the Arapaho chiefs, Left Hand and Little Raven, to disband their camp near Fort Lyon. "Go and hunt buffalo to feed yourselves," he told them. Alarmed by Anthony's abruptness, the Arapahos packed up and began moving away. When they were out of view of the fort, the two bands of Arapahos separated. Left Hand went with his people to Sand Creek to join the Cheyennes. Little Raven led his band across the Arkansas and headed south; he did not trust the new soldier chief.

Anthony now informed his superiors that "there is a band of Indians within forty miles of the post. . . . I shall try to keep the Indians quiet until such time as I receive reinforcements."[11]

On November 27, six hundred men of Colonel Chivington's Colorado regiments arrived at Fort Lyon. When Chivington rode up to the officers' quarters, Major Anthony greeted him warmly. Chivington began talking of "collecting scalps" and "wading in gore." Anthony responded by saying that he had been "waiting for a good chance to pitch into them."[12]

At eight o'clock on the evening of November 28, Chivington's men moved out of the fort. Stars glittered in a clear sky; the night air carried a sharp bite of frost.

At a nearby ranch house Chivington stopped and ordered the rancher hauled out of bed and taken as a guide. This was Robert Bent, oldest son of William Bent; George and Charlie, Bent's other half-breed sons, were already camped with the Cheyennes. All three of them would soon be together at Sand Creek.

The Cheyenne camp lay in a horseshoe bend of Sand Creek. Black Kettle's tepee was near the center, with White Antelope's people to the west. On the east was Left Hand's Arapaho camp. Altogether there were about six hundred Indians in the creek bend, two-thirds of them women and children. Most of the warriors were away hunting buffalo for the camp as they had been told to do by Major Anthony.

The Indians were so confident of safety that they kept no night watch. George Bent was asleep when he heard shouts and the noise of people running.

From down the creek a large body of troops was advancing at a rapid trot . . . in the camps themselves all was confusion and noise—men, women, and children rushing out of the lodges partly dressed; women and children screaming at sight of the troops; men running back into the lodges for their arms. . . . I looked toward the chief's lodge and saw that Black Kettle had a large American flag tied to the end of a long lodgepole and was standing in front of his lodge, holding the pole, with the flag fluttering in the gray light of the winter dawn. I heard him call to the people not to be afraid, that the soldiers would not hurt them; then the troops opened fire from two sides of the camp.[13]

Hundreds of Cheyenne women and children were gathering around Black Kettle's flag. After all, had not Colonel Greenwood told him that as long as the United States flag flew above him no soldier would ever fire upon him? White Antelope, an old man of seventy-five, unarmed, his dark face seamed from sun and weather, strode toward the soldiers. He was still confident that the soldiers would stop firing as soon as they saw the American flag and the white surrender flag which Black Kettle had now run up.

A mulatto whom Chivington had brought along as a guide saw White Antelope approaching. "He came running out to meet the command, holding up his hands and saying 'Stop! Stop!' He spoke it in as plain English as I can. He stopped and folded his arms until shot down."[14] Survivors among the Cheyennes said that White Antelope sang the death song before he died:

> Nothing lives long
> Only the earth and the mountains.

From the direction of the Arapaho camp, Left Hand and his people also tried to reach Black Kettle's flag. When Left Hand saw the troops, he stood with his arms folded, saying he would not fight the white men because they were his friends. He was shot down.

Robert Bent, who was riding unwillingly with the troops, said:

> After the firing the warriors put the squaws and children together, and surrounded them to protect them. I saw five squaws under a bank for shelter. When the troops came up to them they ran out and showed their persons to let the soldiers know they were squaws and begged for mercy, but the soldiers shot them all. I saw one squaw lying on the bank whose leg had been broken by a shell; a soldier came up to her with a drawn saber; she raised her arm to protect herself, when he struck, breaking her arm; she rolled over and raised her other arm, when he struck, breaking it, and then left her without killing her. There seemed to be indiscriminate slaughter of men, women, and children. There were some thirty or forty squaws collected in a hole for protection; they sent out a little girl about six years old with a white flag on a stick; she had not proceeded but a few steps when she was shot and killed. All the squaws in that hole were afterwards killed, and four or five bucks outside. The squaws offered no resistance. Every one I saw dead was scalped. I saw one squaw cut open with an unborn child, as I thought, lying by her side. . . . I saw the body of White Antelope with the privates cut off, and I heard a soldier say he was going to make a tobacco pouch out of them. I saw one squaw whose privates had been cut out. . . . I saw a little girl about five years of age who had been hid in the sand; two soldiers discovered her, drew their pistols and shot her, and then pulled her out of the sand by the arm. I saw quite a number of infants in arms killed with their mothers.[15]

When the shooting ended, 105 Indian women and children and 28 men were dead. Poor discipline, poor marksmanship, and heavy whiskey drinking among the Colorado soldiers made it possible for many Indians to escape. After nightfall

the survivors crawled out of holes they had dug for protection. It was bitter cold, and blood had frozen over their
wounds, but they dared not make fires. The only thought in
their minds was to flee toward the Smoky Hill and try to
join their warriors. "It was a terrible march," George Bent
remembered, "most of us being on foot, without food, ill-
clad, and encumbered with the women and children." At
last they reached the hunting camp. "As we rode into that
camp there was a terrible scene. Everyone was crying, even
the warriors, and the women and children screaming and
wailing. Nearly everyone present had lost some relatives or
friends, and many of them in their grief were gashing themselves with their knives until the blood flowed in streams."[16]

As soon as his wound healed, George went back to his
father's ranch. From his brother Charlie, who had been taken
prisoner at the end of the fighting and then rescued, he heard
more details of the soldiers' atrocities at Sand Creek—the
horrible scalpings and mutilations, the butchery of children
and infants. After a few days the brothers agreed that as
half-breeds they wanted no part of the white man's civiliza-
tion. They renounced the blood of their father and went to
join the Cheyennes.

It was now January, the Moon of Strong Cold, when Plains
Indians traditionally kept fires blazing in their lodges, told
stories through the long evenings, and slept late in the morn-
ings. But this was a bad time. As news of the Sand Creek
massacre spread across the plains, the Cheyennes, Arapahos,
and Sioux sent runners back and forth with messages calling
for a war of revenge against the murdering white men.

In a few hours of madness at Sand Creek, Chivington and his
soldiers destroyed the lives or the power of every Cheyenne
and Arapaho chief who had held out for peace with the

10. *George Bent and his wife, Magpie. Photographed in 1867. Courtesy of State Historical Society of Colorado.*

white men. After the flight of the survivors, the Indians rejected Black Kettle and turned to their war leaders to save them from extermination.

In January 1865, the alliance of Cheyenne, Arapaho, and Sioux launched a series of raids along the South Platte. They attacked wagon trains, stage stations, and military outposts. They burned the town of Julesburg, scalping the white defenders in revenge for the scalping of Indians at Sand Creek. They ripped out miles of telegraph wire, stopping all communications and supplies. In Denver there was panic as food shortages began to grow.

When the warriors returned to their winter camp in the Big Timbers on the Republican, they held a dance to celebrate their first blows for revenge. Snow blanketed the Plains but the chiefs knew that soldiers would soon come marching from all directions with their big-talking guns. While the dances were still going on, the chiefs held a council to decide where they should go to escape from the soldiers. Black Kettle spoke for going south, below the Arkansas, where summers were long and buffalo was plentiful. Some four hundred Cheyennes—mainly old men, women, and a few badly wounded warriors—agreed to go with him. Most of the other chiefs decided to go north across the Platte to join their relatives in the Powder River country. No soldiers would dare march into that great stronghold of the Teton Sioux and Northern Cheyennes.

With about three thousand Arapahos and Sioux, the Cheyennes moved northward, exiled into a land that few of them had seen before. When they reached the Powder River country they were welcomed by their kinsmen, the Northern Cheyennes. The Southerners, who wore cloth blankets and leggings traded from white men, thought the Northerners looked wild in their buffalo robes and buckskin leggings. The

Northern Cheyennes wore crow feathers on their heads, and used so many Sioux words that the Southern Cheyennes had difficulty understanding them. Morning Star, a leading chief of the Northern Cheyennes, had lived and hunted so long with the Sioux that almost everyone called him by his Sioux name, Dull Knife.

At first the Southerners camped on the Powder half a mile from the Northerners, but there was so much visiting back and forth that they soon decided to pitch their tepees in a tribal circle with clans grouped together. From that time on, there was little talk of Southerners and Northerners among these Cheyennes.

In the spring of 1865, when they moved their ponies westward for better grazing, they camped near Red Cloud's Oglala Sioux. The Cheyennes from the South had never seen so many Indians camped all together, more than eight thousand. Although each tribe kept its own laws and customs, they had come to think of themselves as the People, confident of their power and sure of their right to live as they pleased. White invaders were challenging them on the east in Dakota and on the south along the Platte but they were ready to meet all challenges.

Through the springtime the Indians sent scouting parties down to watch the soldiers who were guarding the roads and telegraph lines along the Platte. The scouts reported that the number of soldiers had increased and some were prowling northward. Red Cloud and the other chiefs decided it was time to teach the soldiers a lesson. They would strike them at the point where they were farthest north, a place the white men called Platte Bridge Station.

Because the Cheyenne warriors from the South wanted revenge for relatives massacred at Sand Creek, most of them were invited to go along. Roman Nose of the Dog Soldiers was their leader, and he rode with Red Cloud and Dull Knife. Almost three thousand warriors formed the war party. Among them were the Bent brothers, painted and dressed for battle.

For two days the Indians waited in the hills across from the soldiers and tried unsuccessfully to draw them into open fighting. Then on July 26, to their surprise, a large company of cavalrymen came riding out to meet an approaching wagon train. Several hundred warriors swarmed down upon them and surrounded the wagon train as well. Roman Nose's brother was killed. When Roman Nose heard of this, he was angry for revenge and he called out for all the Cheyennes to prepare for a charge. "We are going to empty the soldiers' guns!" he shouted. Roman Nose was wearing his medicine bonnet and shield, and he knew that no bullets could strike him. He led the Cheyennes into a circle around the wagons, and they lashed their ponies so that they ran very fast. As the circle tightened around the wagons, the soldiers emptied all their guns at once, and then the Cheyennes charged straight for the wagons and killed all the soldiers. They were disappointed by what they found in the wagons: soldiers' bedding and mess chests.

That night, back at camp, Red Cloud and the other chiefs decided they had taught the soldiers to fear the power of the Indians. And so they returned to the Powder River country, hopeful that the white men would stop prowling without permission into the Indians' country north of the Platte.

Meanwhile, Black Kettle and the remaining Southern Cheyennes had moved south of the Arkansas River. They joined Little Raven's Arapahos, who by this time had heard of the Sand Creek massacre and were mourning lost friends and relatives. During the summer of 1865, their hunters found

11. *Wolf Chief, or Honii-wigoi.*
Photographed by DeLancey
Gill, Washington, D.C., 1908.
Courtesy of the Smithsonian
Institution.

12. *White Antelope and unidentified*
person. Photographer not recorded,
but taken between 1900 and 1907.
Courtesy of the Smithsonian
Institution.

13. *Dull Knife. Courtesy of the*
Smithsonian Institution.

14. *Little Raven, chief of the*
Arapahos. Photographer not
recorded, but taken prior
to 1877. Courtesy of the
Smithsonian Institution.

only a few buffalo below the Arkansas. Scarce as food was, they were afraid to go back north.

Late in the summer, runners began coming from all directions looking for Black Kettle and Little Raven, who had suddenly become very important. Some white officials had journeyed from Washington to make a new treaty.

Although the Cheyennes and Arapahos had been driven from Colorado, and settlers were claiming their lands, it seemed that the ownership of the lands was not clear. By the law of the old treaties it could be proved that Denver City itself stood upon Cheyenne and Arapaho land. The government wanted all Indian land claims in Colorado blotted out so that white settlers would be certain they owned the land once they had claimed it.

Black Kettle and Little Raven would not meet with the officials unless the Little White Man, William Bent, was there to protect their interests. At last it was arranged and in the Drying Grass Moon, at the mouth of the Little Arkansas, the treaty meeting began.

"Here we are, all together, Arapahos and Cheyennes," Black Kettle said, "but few of us, we are one people. . . . All my friends, the Indians that are holding back—they are afraid to come in; are afraid they will be betrayed as I have been."

"It will be a very hard thing to leave the country that God gave us," Little Raven said. "Our friends are buried there, and we hate to leave these grounds. . . . This is hard on us. There at Sand Creek—White Antelope and many other chiefs lie there; our women and children lie there. Our lodges were destroyed there, and our horses were taken from us there, and I do not feel disposed to go right off to a new country and leave them."[17]

James Steele, one of the treaty makers, answered the chiefs

gently. He told them that gold had been discovered in their country and many of the white men who had gone there were the worst enemies of the Indians. Nowhere in all that vast land was a place large enough for the Indians to avoid conflict, to live in peace.

And so they agreed to settle south of the Arkansas, sharing land that belonged to the Kiowas. On October 14, 1865, the chiefs and head men of what remained of the Southern Cheyennes and Arapahos signed a new treaty giving up all claims to the Territory of Colorado. The massacre at Sand Creek had accomplished its purpose.

5

Powder River Invasion

The Great Spirit raised both the white man and the Indian.
I think he raised the Indian first. He raised me in this land and
it belongs to me. The white man was raised over the great waters,
and his land is over there. Since they crossed the sea, I have
given them room. There are now white people all about me.
I have but a small spot of land left. The Great Spirit told me to
keep it.
— MAHPIUA LUTA (RED CLOUD) OF THE OGLALA SIOUX

AFTER RETURNING to the Powder River country following
the Platte Bridge fight, the Plains Indians began preparing
for their usual summer medicine ceremonies. The tribes
camped near each other at the mouth of Crazy Woman's
Fork of the Powder. Farther north along that river were
some Teton Sioux who had moved west from Dakota to get
away from pursuing soldiers. Sitting Bull and his Hunkpapa
people were there, and they sent representatives down for a
big sun dance, the annual religious renewal of the Tetons.
While the sun dance was in progress, the Cheyennes held
their medicine-arrow ceremony, which lasted four days. The
Arrow Keeper unwrapped the four secret arrows from their
coyote fur bag, and all the males in the tribe passed by to
make an offering and pray to the arrows.

Black Bear, one of the leading chiefs of the Northern Arapahos, decided to take his people west to Tongue River; he
invited some of the Southern Arapahos who had come north
after Sand Creek to come along. They would set up a village
on the Tongue, he said, and have many hunts and dances before the coming of the cold moons.

During this time in the summer of 1865, the Indians
camped in the Powder River country felt their territory was
secure. On about August 14 or 15 they learned of a large
wagon train accompanied by many soldiers approaching
from the east. Actually, the expedition had been organized
by a civilian, James A. Sawyers, to open up a new route
to the Montana gold fields. Because Sawyers knew that he
could expect resistance for trespassing on Indian treaty lands,
he had obtained the soldiers to escort the miners and their
supply wagons.

But the Cheyennes and Sioux did not know this. Immediately they prepared for battle. George Bent recalled afterward:

> Our hunters rode into camp much excited and said sol-
> diers were up the river. Our village crier, a man named
> Bull Bear, mounted and rode about our camp, crying that
> soldiers were coming. Red Cloud got in his herd and
> mounted and rode through the Sioux camp, crying the
> same thing for the Sioux. Everybody ran for ponies. At
> such times a man always took any pony he wanted; if the
> pony was killed in the fight the rider did not have to pay
> its owner for it, but everything the rider captured in bat-
> tle belonged to the owner of the pony he rode.[1]

About five hundred Sioux and Cheyennes were in the war
party, and both Red Cloud and Dull Knife went along. The
chiefs were very angry that soldiers had come into their
country without asking permission.

When they first saw the wagon train, it was moving along

between two hills with a herd of cattle in the rear. The Indians spread out along opposite ridges and began firing. In a few minutes the train formed into a protective circle with the cattle herded inside.

The Indians could not get at it, but neither could the wagon train move. About midday the chiefs ordered a white flag run up. A meeting was quickly arranged between Red Cloud, Dull Knife, and Colonel Sawyers. The Bent brothers acted as interpreters.

When asked why they had attacked peaceful white men, Charlie Bent, still bitter with memories of Sand Creek, replied that the Cheyennes would fight all white men until the government hanged Colonel Chivington. Sawyers protested that he had not come to fight Indians; he was seeking a short route to the Montana gold fields, and only wanted to pass through the country. They were on their way north along the Powder River valley to find a fort that General Patrick Connor was building there.

This was the first time that Red Cloud and Dull Knife had heard of General Connor and the fort. They expressed surprise and anger that soldiers would dare to build a fort in the heart of their hunting grounds. Seeing that the chiefs were becoming hostile, Sawyers quickly offered them a wagonload of flour, sugar, coffee, and tobacco in exchange for permission to move to Powder River. Finally the Indians agreed to accept it and moved on up the valley to see what they could find out about General Connor and his fort on the Powder.

A month earlier, Connor had come into the country north of the Platte and begun organizing three columns of soldiers for a full-scale invasion. One column had been sent out from Nebraska and one from Fort Laramie with orders to "Attack and kill every male Indian over twelve years of age."[2] They were to link up in the Black Hills and meet the third column,

15. *Red Cloud, or Mahpiua-luta, of the Oglala Dakotas. Photographed by Charles M. Bell in Washington, D.C., in 1880. Courtesy of the Smithsonian Institution.*

with Connor himself in command, on Rosebud River at the beginning of September. General Connor thus hoped to trap the Indians between the combined forces of the three columns.

He spent most of August constructing a stockade sixty miles south of the Crazy Woman's Fork of the Powder and named it Fort Connor in honor of himself. This is where Sawyers' expedition was headed. On August 22 Connor decided that the stockade was strong enough to be held by one company of soldiers. He started off with the rest of his column toward the Tongue River valley in search of Indian villages to destroy.

About a week after Connor's column left the Powder, a Cheyenne warrior named Little Horse was traveling across this same country with his Arapaho wife and young son. They were making a summer visit to relatives in Black Bear's Arapaho camp on Tongue River. Along the way one day, Little Horse's wife happened to glance back across a ridge. A file of mounted soldiers was coming far behind them.

Little Horse cut loose the travois on which his young son was riding, took the boy on behind him, and they rode fast —straight across country for Black Bear's camp. They came galloping in, disturbing the peaceful village of some two hundred and fifty lodges pitched on a mesa above the river. The Arapahos were rich in ponies that year; three thousand were corralled along the stream.

None of the Arapahos believed that soldiers could be within hundreds of miles. Not even Little Horse's relatives would listen. "You saw nothing but some buffalo," his wife's brother said. Only a few people decided to come with them, and before nightfall they had left the village and moved several miles down the Tongue for safety.[3]

Early the next morning, Star Chief Connor's soldiers attacked the Arapaho camp. As soon as they realized they were in danger, the Indians tried to scatter their three thousand ponies along the river valley. The village, which had been peaceful and quiet a few minutes before, suddenly became a scene of fearful uproar—horses rearing and whinnying, dogs barking, women screaming, children crying, warriors and soldiers yelling and cursing.

In the first moments of battle, some women and children were caught between the warriors and the cavalrymen. "I was in the village in the midst of a hand-to-hand fight with warriors and their squaws," said one of Connor's officers, "for many of the female portion of this band did as brave fighting as their savage lords. Unfortunately for the women and children, our men had no time to direct their aim . . . squaws and children, as well as warriors, fell among the dead and wounded."[4]

As quickly as they could catch ponies, the Arapahos mounted and began retreating. The soldiers pressed close behind for ten miles but when their horses became tired, the warriors turned on them. By early afternoon Connor's troops had been driven back to the village, but artillerymen had mounted two howitzers there, and the big-talking guns filled the air with whistling pieces of metal. The Arapahos could go no farther.

While they watched from the hills, the soldiers tore down all the lodges in the village and heaped buffalo robes, blankets, furs, and thirty tons of pemmican into great mounds and set fire to them. Everything the Arapahos owned—shelter, clothing, and their winter supply of food—went up in smoke. The soldiers mounted and left with the thousand ponies they had captured, one-third of the tribe's herd.

During the afternoon, Little Horse heard the big guns in his hiding place down the river. As soon as the soldiers left, he and his wife and those who had heeded their warning came back into the burned village. They found more than fifty dead Indians; many others were badly wounded and dying. The Arapahos had nothing left except the ponies they had saved from capture, a few weapons, and the clothing they were wearing when the soldiers charged into the village. This was the Battle of Tongue River that happened in the Moon When the Geese Shed Their Feathers.

Star Chief Connor meanwhile headed north toward the Rosebud where he had arranged to meet the other two columns sent out in July. His scouts searched in all directions but could find no trace of either column. It was already September 8. They were a week overdue.

On August 18 the two columns had linked up in the Black Hills as planned. Morale was low among the two thousand soldiers. Rations were so short that they began slaughtering mules for meat. Scurvy broke out among the men. Because of a shortage of grass and water, their mounts grew weaker and weaker. With men and horses in such condition, neither of the two officers in command wanted to fight the Indians. Their only objective was to reach the Rosebud for the meeting with General Connor.

As for the Indians, there were thousands of them in the sacred places of Paha-Sapa, the Black Hills. It was summer, the time for communing with the Great Spirit and seeking visions. Members of all tribes were there at the center of the world, engaged in religious ceremonies. They watched the dust streamers of two thousand soldiers and hated them for their desecration of Paha-Sapa. But no war parties were formed and the Indians kept away from the noisy, dusty procession.

On August 28 when they reached the Powder, the two

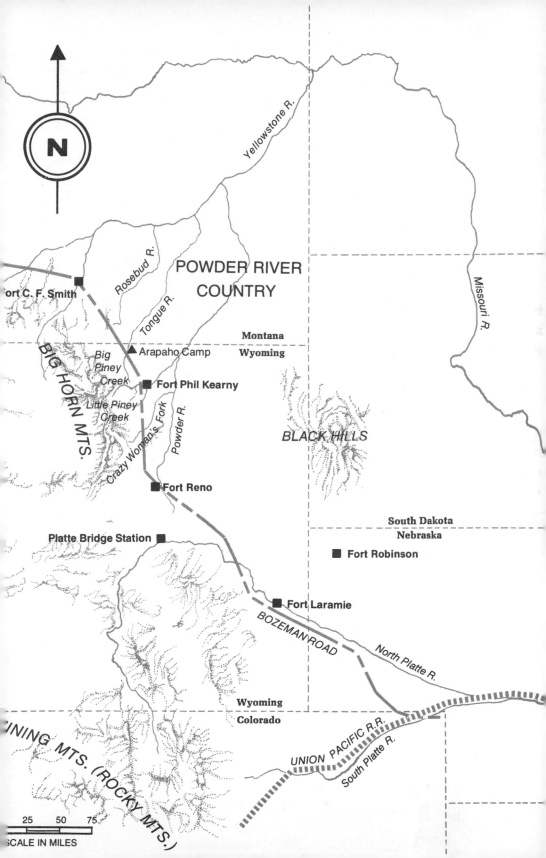

commanders sent scouts ahead to the Rosebud to look for General Connor, but he was still far to the south that day preparing to destroy Black Bear's Arapaho village.

During the few days that the soldiers were camped on the Powder, they were discovered by bands of Hunkpapa and Minneconjou Sioux. With them was the Hunkpapa leader, Sitting Bull. Some of the young Sioux warriors wanted to ride in under a truce flag and persuade the Bluecoats to give them tobacco and sugar as peace offerings. Sitting Bull did not trust white men and was against such begging, but he held back and let the others send a truce party down toward the camp.

The soldiers allowed the Sioux truce party to approach, then fired, killing and wounding several of them. On their way back the survivors made off with several horses from the soldiers' herd.

Sitting Bull was not surprised at the way the soldiers had treated their peaceful Indian visitors. After looking at the skinny horses taken from the soldiers' herd, he decided that four hundred Sioux on fast ponies should be an equal match for two thousand soldiers on half-starved army mounts.

The Sioux rode down to the camp single file, circled the soldiers guarding the horse herd, and began picking them off one by one. Then a company of cavalrymen came charging up the bank of the Powder. The Sioux quickly withdrew on their fast ponies, easily keeping out of rifle range. Three times the soldiers charged and three times the Sioux scattered and defeated them.

Alarmed by the Indian attack, the commanders of the two columns decided to give up the idea of meeting Connor and instead moved southward. For a few days the Sioux followed the soldiers, scaring them by appearing suddenly. Sitting Bull and the other leaders laughed at how frightened the Bluecoats became, looking over their shoulders and hurrying away.

Then there was a big sleet storm and the Indians took shelter for two days. One morning they heard scattered firing from the direction in which the soldiers had gone. The next day the Sioux found their abandoned camp. The ground was covered with dead horses, nine hundred of them. They could see that the horses had been covered with sheets of freezing rain. The soldiers had shot them because they could make them go no farther.

Since many of the frightened Bluecoats were now on foot, the Sioux decided to drive them so crazy with fear that they would never return to the Black Hills again. Along the way these Hunkpapas and Minneconjous began meeting small scouting parties of Oglala Sioux and Cheyennes. There was great excitement in these meetings. Only a few miles south was a big Cheyenne village, and as runners brought the leaders of the bands together, they began planning a big ambush for the soldiers.

During that summer Roman Nose had made many medicine fasts for protection against enemies. Like Red Cloud and Sitting Bull, he was determined to fight for his country, and he was also determined to win. White Bull, an old Cheyenne medicine man, advised him to go alone to a lake nearby and live with the water spirits. For four days Roman Nose lay on a raft in the lake without food or water, enduring the hot sun by day and thunderstorms at night. He prayed to the Great Spirit and to the water spirits. After Roman Nose returned to camp, White Bull made him a protective war bonnet with so many eagle feathers that when he was mounted, the war bonnet trailed almost to the ground.

In September, when the Cheyenne camp first heard about the soldiers fleeing south up the Powder, Roman Nose asked to lead a charge against the Bluecoats. A day or two later the soldiers were camped in a bend of the river with high bluffs on both sides. The chiefs decided that this was an excellent place for an attack and positioned several hundred warriors all around the camp.

Now Roman Nose rode up on his white pony, his war bonnet trailing behind him, his face painted for battle. He called to the warriors not to fight singly as they had always done but to fight together in a line as the soldiers did. Then he slapped his pony into a run and rode straight as an arrow down the soldiers' line. They emptied their guns at him all along the way.

"He made three, or perhaps four, rushes from one end of the line to the other," said George Bent. "And then his pony was shot and fell under him. On seeing this, the warriors set up a yell and charged. They attacked the troops all along the line, but could not break through anywhere."[5]

Roman Nose had lost his horse, but his protective medicine saved his life. He also learned some things that day about fighting Bluecoats—and so did Red Cloud, Sitting Bull, Dull Knife, and the other leaders. Bravery, numbers, massive charges—they all meant nothing if the warriors were armed only with bows, lances, and a few old guns.

For several days after the fight—which would be remembered as Roman Nose's fight—the Cheyennes and Sioux continued to harass the soldiers. The Bluecoats were now barefoot and in rags, and had no food. Finally they ate their bony horses raw because they were too rushed to build fires. At last in the Drying Grass Moon toward the end of September, Star Chief Connor's column returned to rescue the other two columns of beaten soldiers. The soldiers all camped together around Fort Connor until orders came from Fort Laramie calling back the majority of them.

16. *Sitting Bull. Photo from the U.S. Signal Corps.*

The troops that stayed on through the winter were left with six howitzers to defend the stockade. Red Cloud and the other leaders decided that if they tried to take Fort Connor, too many warriors would die by the big guns. They finally agreed to keep a constant watch on the fort and blockade its supply trail from Fort Laramie. They would hold the soldiers prisoners in their own fort and cut off their supplies.

Before that winter ended, half the luckless troops that remained behind were dead or dying of scurvy, malnutrition, and pneumonia. Many slipped away and deserted, taking their chances outside with the Indians.

As for the Indians, all except the small bands needed to watch the fort moved over to the Black Hills, where plentiful herds of antelope and buffalo kept them fat in their warm lodges. Through the long winter evenings the chiefs recounted the events of Star Chief Connor's invasion. Because the Arapahos had been overconfident and careless, they had lost a village, several lives, and part of their rich pony herd. The other tribes had lost a few lives but no horses or lodges. They had captured many horses and mules carrying U.S. brands. They had taken many carbines, saddles, and other equipment from the soldiers. Above all, they had gained a new confidence in their ability to drive the Bluecoat soldiers from their country.

"If white men come into my country again, I will punish them again," Red Cloud said. But he knew that unless he could somehow obtain many new guns like the ones the soldiers used and plenty of ammunition, the Indians could not go on punishing the soldiers forever.

6

Red Cloud's War

This war did not spring up here in our land; this war was brought upon us by the children of the Great Father who came to take our land from us without price, and who, in our land, do a great many evil things. The Great Father and his children are to blame for this trouble. . . . It has been our wish to live here in our country peaceably, and do such things as may be for the welfare and good of our people, but the Great Father has filled it with soldiers who think only of our death.
— SINTE-GALESHKA (SPOTTED TAIL) OF THE BRULÉ SIOUX

IN LATE SUMMER AND AUTUMN of 1865, while the Indians of the Powder River country were demonstrating their military power, a United States treaty commission was traveling along the upper Missouri River. At every Sioux village they handed out blankets, molasses, crackers, and other presents and had no difficulty persuading the Indians to sign new treaties. Yet the commissioners knew very well that without the signatures of Red Cloud and the other war leaders, the treaties would be meaningless.

The white man's Civil War had ended, and white settlers were moving to the West in great numbers. What the treaty makers wanted was the right to build trails, roads, and eventually railroads across the Powder River country. The Bozeman Road was the most important route out of Fort Laramie to Montana. It could not be developed, however, because the warrior chiefs kept up a steady blockade of the trail.

Military officials at Fort Laramie were being pressed by the government to make the Bozeman Road safe for travel. One of the company commanders, Colonel Henry Maynadier, decided to send five Sioux into the Powder River country to find Red Cloud.

The Indians were out for two months, spreading the news that fine presents awaited all warrior chiefs who would come in to Fort Laramie and sign new treaties. In January 1866, they returned with two destitute bands of Brulé Sioux eager to receive the clothing and provisions that had been promised. Spotted Tail, the head man of the Brulés, would come in as soon as his daughter was able to travel. She was ill of the coughing sickness.

"But what about Red Cloud?" Colonel Maynadier wanted to know. Where were Red Cloud, Young-Man-Afraid-of-His-Horses, Dull Knife—the leaders who had fought Connor's soldiers? The Sioux messengers assured him that the warrior chiefs would be there in a short time. They could not be hurried, especially in the Moon of Strong Cold.

Weeks passed, and then early in March, word came that Spotted Tail, the Brulé chief, was coming to discuss the treaty. He hoped that the soldiers' doctor could make his daughter well again. A few days later, when Maynadier learned that the girl had died, he turned it into an occasion for diplomacy. A company of soldiers and an ambulance were immediately sent out to meet the mourning procession of Brulés. When they reached the fort, the entire garrison was there to honor them.

Maynadier invited Spotted Tail into his headquarters and offered sympathy for the loss of his daughter. The chief said that in the days when the white men and the Indians were at peace, he had brought his daughter to Fort Laramie many times, that she had loved the fort, and he would like to have

17. *Spotted Tail, or Sinte-Galeshka, of the Brulé Sioux. From a painting by Henry Ulke made in 1877, now in the National Portrait Gallery of the Smithsonian Institution.*

her buried in the post cemetery. Colonel Maynadier immediately granted permission. He would arrange a military funeral for her the following day. The colonel was surprised to see tears well up in Spotted Tail's eyes; he did not know that an Indian could weep. Somewhat awkwardly he changed the subject. The Great Father was sending out a new peace commission in the spring; he hoped that Spotted Tail could stay near the fort until the commissioners arrived; there was a great urgency to open up the Bozeman Road.

"We think we have been very much wronged," Spotted Tail replied, "and are entitled to compensation for the damage and distress caused by making so many roads through our country, and driving off and destroying the buffalo and game. My heart is very sad, and I cannot talk on business; I will wait and see the counselors the Great Father will send."[1]

Five days later Red Cloud and a large party of Oglalas appeared suddenly outside the fort. They stopped first at Spotted Tail's camp, and the two Sioux leaders were enjoying a reunion when Maynadier came out to conduct both of them to his headquarters with the pomp and ceremony of an Army band.

When Maynadier told Red Cloud that the new peace commission would not arrive at the fort for some weeks, the Oglala chief became angry. The Sioux messengers had told him that if he came in and signed a treaty, he would receive presents. He needed guns and powder and provisions. Maynadier invited Red Cloud to send a message over the telegraph to the president of the new commission. When the reply came back over the talking wires promising a train loaded with supplies and presents to arrive at Fort Laramie by the first of June, Red Cloud was satisfied. He would wait until the Moon When the Green Grass Is Up for the treaty signing.

As a goodwill gesture, Maynadier gave small amounts of powder and lead to the Oglalas, and they rode away in fine good humor. Nothing had been said by Maynadier about opening the Bozeman Road; the subject could be postponed until the treaty council.

When Red Cloud returned to Fort Laramie he brought with him his chief lieutenant, Young-Man-Afraid-of-His-Horses, and more than a thousand Oglalas; Dull Knife came with several lodges of Cheyennes, and together with Spotted Tail's people and the other Brulés they formed a great camp along the Platte River.

Unfortunately for the peace commissioners, Colonel Henry B. Carrington and seven hundred soldiers arrived near Fort Laramie on June 13, just as the treaty meetings were beginning. They had marched from Nebraska, and were under orders to build a chain of forts along the Bozeman Road in preparation for the expected heavy travel to Montana during the summer. None of the Indians invited to the treaty signing had been told anything about this military occupation of the Powder River country.

Standing Elk, one of the Brulé chiefs, watched from his distant tepee while the soldiers formed their wagon train into a square. He then rode over to the camp and asked to see Colonel Carrington. After they had gone through the formalities of pipe smoking, Standing Elk asked bluntly: "Where are you going?"

Carrington replied that he was taking his troops to the Powder River country to guard the road to Montana.

"There is a treaty being made in Laramie with the Sioux that are in the country where you are going," Standing Elk told him. "You will have to fight the Sioux warriors if you go there."[2]

By the next day's treaty meetings, the presence and purpose of Carrington's regiment were known to every Indian at Fort Laramie. In Red Cloud's speech to the peace commissioners, he scolded them for treating the Indians like children, for pretending to negotiate for a country while they prepared to take it by conquest. "The white men have crowded the Indians back year by year," he said, "until we are forced to live in a small country north of the Platte, and now our last hunting ground, the home of the People, is to be taken from us. Our women and children will starve, but for my part I prefer to die fighting rather than by starvation. . . . Great Father sends us presents and wants new road. But White Chief goes with soldiers to steal road before Indian says yes or no!" While the interpreter was still translating the Sioux words into English, the listening Indians became so disorderly that the commissioners abruptly ended the meeting. Red Cloud strode past them as if they were not there, and continued on toward the Oglala camp. Before the next dawn, the Oglalas were gone from Fort Laramie.[3] The war which the treaty commission wanted to end had instead been given new momentum.

During the next few weeks, as Carrington's wagon train moved north along the Bozeman Road, the Indians had an opportunity to study its size and strength. The two hundred wagons were loaded with mowing machines, shingle and brick machines, rocking chairs, churns, canned goods, and vegetable seeds, as well as the usual ammunition, gunpowder, and other military supplies. The Bluecoats evidently expected to stay in the Powder River country; a number of them had brought their wives and children along.

By June 28 the regiment reached Fort Connor (now renamed Fort Reno), relieving the soldiers who had been kept virtual prisoners there during the winter and spring. Carrington left about one-fourth of his men to protect the post, and then moved on north, searching for a place to build a second stockade.

On July 13 the column stopped between the forks of the Little Piney and Big Piney creeks. There in the heart of a rich grassland near the Bighorn Mountains, on the best hunting grounds of the Plains Indians, the Bluecoats pitched their tents and began building Fort Phil Kearny.

Three days later a large party of Cheyennes approached the camp. Two Moon, Black Horse, and Dull Knife were among the leaders. Under truce flags the Cheyennes arranged a meeting with the Little White Chief Carrington. While the pipe smoking and preliminary speeches were going on, the chiefs studied the power of the soldiers.

Before they were ready to leave, Carrington shot off one of his howitzers for them. The power of the big gun impressed the Indians, as he had hoped it would. A few hours later, villages along the Tongue and Powder heard from the Cheyennes that the new fort was too strong to be captured without great loss. They would have to lure the soldiers out into the open, where they could be more easily attacked.

Next morning at dawn, a band of Red Cloud's Oglalas stampeded 175 mules and horses from Carrington's herd. When the soldiers came riding in pursuit, the Indians strung them out in a fifteen-mile chase and struck the first blows against these new Bluecoat invaders of the Powder River country.

From that day all through the summer of 1866, the Little White Chief was engaged in a relentless guerrilla war. None of the many wagon trains, civilian or military, that moved along the Bozeman Road was safe from surprise attacks.

Red Cloud was everywhere, and his allies increased until the fighting force numbered three thousand. Black Bear, the Arapaho chief whose village had been destroyed by General

Connor the previous summer, joined the fighting with his warriors. Spotted Tail, still believing in peace, had gone to hunt buffalo along the Republican, but many of his Brulés came north. Sitting Bull was there and so was a young Oglala named Crazy Horse.

Though they had a small supply of rifles and ammunition, the majority of warriors were still armed only with bows and arrows. During the early autumn Red Cloud and the other chiefs agreed that they must concentrate their power against the Little White Chief Carrington and the hated fort on the Piney creeks. And so, before the coming of the Cold Moons they moved toward the Bighorns and made their camps along the headwaters of the Tongue. From there they were in easy striking distance of Fort Phil Kearny.

By the third week in December everything was ready, and about two thousand Sioux, Cheyenne, and Arapaho warriors began the journey into battle. The weather was very cold, and they wore buffalo robes with the hair turned in, leggings of dark woolen cloth, and buffalo-fur moccasins. Most of them rode pack horses, leading their fast-footed war ponies by lariats. They carried enough pemmican to last several days. Small groups occasionally would turn off the trail, kill a deer, and take as much meat as could be carried on their saddles.

On the morning of December 21, the chiefs and medicine men decided the day was favorable for a victory. In the first gray light of dawn, the main body of warriors moved down the Bozeman Road and began laying a great ambush along a narrow ridge three miles from the fort. The Cheyennes and Arapahos hid on one side and the Sioux hid on the other. The strategy of battle was this: a small war party would make a false attack against the woodcutters. Ten well-trained decoys would then anger and confuse the soldiers who came to their defense. The soldiers would chase the decoys and be led by them directly into the ambush.

Everything went as planned. At the first sound of gunfire, a company of soldiers led by Captain William J. Fetterman galloped out of the fort to rescue the woodcutters. The decoys, led by Crazy Horse, scattered, jumping and yelling to make the soldiers believe they were frightened. In a few minutes the soldiers came in pursuit.

Crazy Horse and the other decoys now jumped on their ponies and began riding back and forth, taunting the soldiers and angering them so that they fired recklessly. When the soldiers slowed their advance or halted, Crazy Horse would dismount and pretend to adjust his bridle. Bullets whined all around him and then the soldiers began to chase the decoys down to the place of ambush. They were the only Indians in sight—only ten of them—and the soldiers were charging their horses to catch them.

When all eighty-one of the soldiers were within the trap, the signal to attack was given. From the west side of the ridge hundreds of mounted Cheyennes and Arapahos charged with a sudden thunder of hooves. From the opposite side came the Sioux. For a few minutes the Indians and the walking soldiers were mixed in confused hand-to-hand fighting. The infantrymen were soon all killed but the mounted soldiers retreated up a hillside near the end of the ridge and had to be chased in bloody battle.

Toward the end of the fighting, the Cheyennes and Arapahos on one side and the Sioux on the other were so close together that they began hitting each other with their arrows. Then it was all over. Not a soldier was left alive. A dog came out from among the dead, and a Sioux started to catch it to take home with him, but Big Rascal, a Cheyenne, said, "Don't let the dog go," and somebody shot it with an arrow. This was the fight the white men called the Fetterman Massacre; the Indians called it the Battle of the Hundred Slain.[4]

Now it was the Moon of Strong Cold, and there would be no more fighting for a while. The soldiers who were left alive in the fort would have a bitter taste of defeat in their mouths. If they had not learned their lesson and were still there when the grass greened in the spring, the war would continue.

The Fetterman Massacre made a profound impression upon Colonel Carrington. He was shocked by the mutilations—the disembowelings, the hacked limbs, the "private parts severed and indecently placed on the person." He decided finally that the Indians were compelled by some paganistic beliefs to commit such terrible deeds. But if Colonel Carrington had visited the scene of the Sand Creek Massacre, which occurred only two years earlier, he would have seen the same mutilations—committed upon Indians by white soldiers.

The Fetterman Massacre also made a profound impression upon the United States government. It was the worst defeat the Army had ever suffered in Indian warfare. Carrington was immediately removed from command, and a new peace commission was sent from Washington to Fort Laramie in April 1867.

This second attempt to end the fighting in the Powder River country by means of treaty was a complete failure. Once again, Spotted Tail came in with his Brulés and spoke for friendship and peace with the white men. For this he received enough powder and lead for the summer buffalo hunts. Young-Man-Afraid-of-His-Horses arrived as a representative for Red Cloud and told the commissioners that the Oglala chief would not talk about peace until all soldiers were taken out of the Powder River country.

18. *Young-Man-Afraid-of-His-Horses. Courtesy of the Nebraska State Historical Society.*

The Indians were more determined than ever before to keep their last great hunting ground. The Union Pacific Railroad was being built across western Nebraska and the Iron Horse that ran on the iron tracks was frightening all the game out of the Platte valley.

In their search for buffalo and antelope, the Oglalas and Cheyennes crossed the railroad tracks several times that summer. Sometimes they saw Iron Horses dragging wooden houses on wheels at great speeds along the tracks. They puzzled over what could be inside the houses.

One day a Cheyenne named Sleeping Rabbit decided to catch one of the Iron Horses and find out. "If we could bend the track up and spread it out, the Iron Horse might fall off," he said. His plan worked. When the engine came, it fell over on its side, and smoke came out of it. Men ran from the train, and the Indians killed all but two, who escaped and ran away. They then broke open the houses on wheels and found sacks of flour, sugar, and coffee, and boxes of whiskey. They drank some of the whiskey and began tying bolts of cloth to their ponies' tails. The ponies went dashing off across the prairie with long streamers of cloth unrolling behind them. After a while the Indians took hot coals from the wrecked engine and set the boxcars on fire. Then they rode away before soldiers could come to punish them.[5]

Incidents such as this, combined with Red Cloud's continuing war, which had brought civilian travel to an end through the Powder River country, had a strong effect on the United States government. It was determined to protect the route of the Union Pacific Railroad, but some officials thought that perhaps the Powder River country should be left to the Indians in return for peace along the Platte valley.

Late in July, after holding their sun-dance and medicine-arrow ceremonies, the Sioux and Cheyennes decided to wipe out one of the forts on the Bozeman Road. The two tribes could not decide which fort to attack. Finally, they reached an agreement: the Sioux would attack Fort Phil Kearny; the Cheyennes went ninety miles north to Fort C. F. Smith, the third and newest post.

On August 1 five or six hundred Cheyenne warriors caught thirty soldiers in a hayfield about two miles from Fort C. F. Smith. Unknown to the Indians, the defenders were armed with new Springfield repeating rifles, and when they charged the soldiers' log corral they met such a withering fire that only one warrior was able to get through, and he was killed. The Cheyennes then set fire to the high, dry grass, carried their dead and wounded away under cover of the smoke, and started back south to see if the Sioux had found better luck at Fort Phil Kearny.

The Sioux had not. The decoy trick which had worked so well with Captain Fetterman was unsuccessful because the warriors in the ambush came out of hiding too early and warned the soldiers of their presence.

To save something from the fight, Red Cloud then turned the attack against the woodcutters, who had taken cover behind a corral of wagon beds and logs. But as at Fort C. F. Smith, the defenders were armed with Springfield rifles. Faced with rapid and continuous fire from these weapons, the Sioux quickly pulled their ponies away. "Then we left our horses in a gulch and charged on foot," a warrior named Fire Thunder said afterward, "but it was like green grass withering in a fire. So we picked up our wounded and went away. I do not know how many of our people were killed, but there were very many. It was bad."[6]

The two skirmishes were called the Hayfield and Wagon Box fights by white men, who created a great many legends around them. One imaginative writer described the wagon boxes as being ringed by the bodies of dead Indians; although fewer than a thousand Indians were present, casualties were reported at 1,137.

Some soldiers may have regarded these fights as victories but the United States government did not. Only a few weeks later, General William T. Sherman was traveling westward with a new peace council. This time the military authorities were determined to end Red Cloud's war by any method except surrender.

In late summer of 1867, word was sent out to the Plains chiefs that the Great Warrior Sherman was coming with a new peace commission sometime during the Drying Grass Moon. The chiefs would receive presents of ammunition and were to assemble at the end of the Union Pacific Railroad track, which was then in western Nebraska.

Most of the chiefs who responded to the invitation were Brulés and Cheyennes who made their homes on the plains of Nebraska and Kansas. Although Red Cloud was sent for, he refused again, sending Young-Man-Afraid to represent him.

On September 19 a shiny railroad car arrived at Platte City station, the peace commission got off, and the meetings began. Spotted Tail was the first Indian to speak: "The Great Father has made roads stretching east and west. Those roads are the cause of all our troubles. . . . The country where we live is overrun by whites. All our game is gone. This is the cause of great trouble. I have been a friend of the whites, and am now. . . . If you stop your roads we can get our game. That Powder River country belongs to the Sioux. . . . My friends, help us; take pity on us."

All through that first day's meeting, the other chiefs echoed Spotted Tail's words. Although few of these Indians considered the Powder River country as their territory, all supported Red Cloud's determination to keep that last great hunting ground.

On the following day the Great Warrior Sherman addressed the chiefs, blandly assuring them that he had been thinking of their request all night and was ready to give a reply. He said that as long as Red Cloud continued to make war on the forts along the Bozeman Road the soldiers would not leave them. The commissioners would hold another meeting at Fort Laramie in November to examine new developments.

Sherman began to talk about the Indians' need for land of their own, advised them to give up their dependence upon wild game, and then dropped a thunderbolt: "We therefore propose to let the whole Sioux nation select their country up the Missouri River, embracing the White Earth and Cheyenne rivers, to have their lands like the white people, forever. . . ."[7]

As these words were translated, the Indians expressed surprise, murmuring among themselves. So this was what the new commissioners wanted them to do! Pack up and move far away to the Missouri River? For years the Teton Sioux had been following wild game westward from there; why should they go back to the Missouri to starve? Why could they not live in peace where game could still be found? Had the greedy eyes of the white men already chosen these bountiful lands for their own?

Young-Man-Afraid-of-His-Horses lost no time in bringing the news to Red Cloud. If Red Cloud ever had any intention of meeting with the new peace commissioners, he changed his mind after hearing about the Great Warrior Sherman's plan for moving the Sioux nation to the Missouri River.

On November 9, when the commissioners arrived at Fort Laramie, they found only a few Crow chiefs waiting to meet with them. Several days later, messengers arrived from Red Cloud. He would come to talk peace as soon as the troops left the forts on the Bozeman Road. The war, he said, was being fought for one purpose—to save the valley of the Powder, the only hunting ground left his nation, from being taken over by white men. "The Great Father sent his soldiers out here to spill blood. I did not first commence the spilling of blood. . . . If the Great Father kept white men out of my country, peace would last forever, but if they disturb me, there will be no peace. . . . The Great Spirit raised me in this land, and has raised you in another land. What I have said I mean. I mean to keep this land."[8]

For the third time in two years a peace commission had failed. Before the commissioners returned to Washington they made one more effort. They sent Red Cloud a shipment of tobacco with a plea to come to Laramie as soon as the winter snows melted. Red Cloud replied politely, saying he had received the tobacco of peace and would smoke it, and that he would come to Laramie as soon as the soldiers left his country.

In the spring of 1868 the Great Warrior Sherman and the same peace commission returned to Fort Laramie. This time they had firm orders from an impatient government to abandon the forts on the Bozeman Road and make a peace treaty with Red Cloud. A special agent was sent to invite the Oglala leader to a peace signing. Red Cloud told him he would need to talk with his allies and would probably come to Laramie in May, the Moon When the Ponies Shed.

Only a few days after the agent returned to Laramie, however, a message arrived from Red Cloud: "We are on the mountains looking down on the soldiers and the forts. When we see the soldiers moving away and the forts abandoned, then I will come down and talk."[9]

All through the spring and summer of 1868 Red Cloud and his allies remained on the Powder, keeping watch on the forts and the road to Montana. At last the reluctant War Department sent out orders for the abandonment of the Powder River country. On July 29 the troops at Fort C. F. Smith packed their gear and started moving southward. Early the next morning Red Cloud led a band of celebrating warriors into the post, where they set fire to every building. A month later Fort Phil Kearny was abandoned, and the honor of burning was given to the Cheyennes. A few days after that, the last soldier left Fort Reno and the Bozeman Road was officially closed.

After two years of resistance Red Cloud had won his war. For a few more weeks he kept the treaty makers waiting, and then on November 6, surrounded by a group of triumphant warriors, he came riding into Fort Laramie. Now a conquering hero, he would sign the treaty: "From this day forward all war between the parties to this agreement shall forever cease. The government of the United States desires peace, and its honor is hereby pledged to keep it. The Indians desire peace, and they now pledge their honor to maintain it."

For the next twenty years, however, the specific terms of that treaty of 1868 would be argued between the Indians and the government of the United States. What many of the chiefs understood to be in the treaty and what was actually written down after Congress ratified it were like two horses of different colors.

7

"The Only
Good Indian Is a
Dead Indian"

Are not women and children more timid than men? The Cheyenne warriors are not afraid, but have you never heard of Sand Creek? Your soldiers look just like those who butchered the women and children there.
—WOQUINI (ROMAN NOSE) TO GENERAL WINFIELD SCOTT HANCOCK

IN THE SPRING of 1866, as Red Cloud was preparing to fight for the Powder River country, a large number of homesick Southern Cheyennes who had been with him decided to go south for the summer. They wanted to hunt buffalo again along their beloved Smoky Hill and hoped to see some of their old friends and relatives who had gone with Black Kettle below the Arkansas. Among the returning Cheyennes were the two half-breed Bent brothers, the Dog Soldier Chiefs Tall Bull, White Horse, and Bull Bear, and the great war leader Roman Nose.

In the valley of the Smoky Hill they found several bands of young Cheyennes and Arapahos who had slipped away from the camps of Black Kettle and Little Raven. When the chiefs signed the treaty of 1865 after the Sand Creek massacre they had given up tribal rights to these old hunting grounds. Roman Nose and the Dog Soldier chiefs scoffed at the treaty; none of them had signed it, and none accepted it. Fresh from the freedom and independence of the Powder River country, they had no use for chiefs who signed away tribal lands.

By late summer the Indians who were camped along the Smoky Hill began hearing rumors of Red Cloud's successes against the soldiers. If the Sioux and Northern Cheyennes could fight a war to hold their country, then why shouldn't the Southern Cheyennes and Arapahos fight to hold their country between the Smoky Hill and Republican rivers?

With Roman Nose as a unifying leader, many bands came together, and the chiefs made plans to stop travel along the Smoky Hill road. But the snowstorms fell early that year. Faced with a long winter, the Dog Soldiers decided to make permanent camp in the Big Timbers on the Republican and wait to attack in the spring of 1867.

Edward Wynkoop, the Southern Cheyennes' old friend, was now the agent for Black Kettle's people. He wanted the Dog Soldiers to give up the idea of fighting against the Blue-coats and join Black Kettle. Even though the chiefs refused, Tall Chief Wynkoop continued to try to help them as best he could. When he learned that some fourteen hundred soldiers were marching west across the Kansas plains toward Fort Larned, he sent runners to tell the Dog Soldier leaders. Perhaps a truce could be worked out with the commanding officer, General Winfield Scott Hancock.

Fourteen chiefs agreed to come to Fort Larned. When they rode in, General Hancock greeted them in a haughty manner, letting them see the power of his forces, including the new 7th Cavalry. This was commanded by General George Armstrong Custer. The Indians had earlier named him Hard Backsides because he chased them over long distances without leaving his saddle.

Although their friend Tall Chief Wynkoop was there, the Dog Soldier leaders were suspicious of Hancock from the beginning. Instead of waiting until the next day to talk, he called them to a night council. They considered this a bad sign, to hold council at night.

Hancock immediately asked why there weren't more chiefs at the meeting. He was especially annoyed that Roman Nose had not come. "If Roman Nose will not come to me I will go to see him. I will march my troops to your village tomorrow," he said. The Cheyennes were disturbed by this. Their women and children were back in camp, thirty-five miles away at Pawnee Creek; many were survivors of the horrors of Sand Creek three years before. Would Hancock bring his soldiers and his thundering guns down upon them?

As soon as the meeting was over, Tall Bull went to Wynkoop and begged him to stop Hancock. Tall Bull was afraid that if the Bluecoats came near the camp, trouble would erupt between them and the hot-headed young Dog Soldiers.

Wynkoop agreed. "Previous to General Hancock's departure, I expressed to him my fears of the result of his marching his troops immediately on to the Indian village; but, notwithstanding, he persisted in doing so." According to Wynkoop, Hancock's column "had as formidable an aspect and presented as warlike an appearance as any that ever marched to meet an enemy on a battlefield."[1]

For almost two days, the Cheyennes were able to keep the troops away by promising Hancock that Roman Nose would meet with him in council. But on April 14, the Moon of the Red Grass Appearing, Hancock refused to be put off any longer.

When the Indians learned that Hancock's soldiers were

coming, the camp reacted immediately. "I will ride out alone and kill this Hancock!" Roman Nose shouted. The women and children were put on ponies and sent racing northward. Then all the warriors took their weapons and rode out across the plain. Although the chiefs named Roman Nose their war leader, they told Bull Bear to ride beside him to make sure that in his anger he did nothing foolish.

In a few minutes they saw Hancock's column coming. Roman Nose signaled the warriors to stop and raised a truce flag. At this the soldiers slowed their horses. A high wind made the flags and pennants snap along both lines.

Roman Nose drew up near the officers; he sat on his horse facing General Hancock and looked him straight in the eyes.

"Do you want peace or war?" Hancock asked.

"We do not want war," Roman Nose replied. "If we did, we would not come so close to your big guns."

Bull Bear spoke next, asking the general not to bring his soldiers any nearer to the Indian camp. "We have not been able to hold our women and children," he said. "They are frightened and have run away and they will not come back. They fear the soldiers."

"You must get them back," Hancock ordered harshly, "and I expect you to do so."

When Bull Bear turned away with a gesture of frustration, Roman Nose spoke softly to him. "I'm going to kill Hancock," he said. Bull Bear grabbed the bridle of Roman Nose's horse and led him aside, warning him that such an action would surely bring death to all the tribe. Roman Nose finally became calmer.

The wind had come up, blowing sand and making conversation difficult. After ordering the chiefs to start out immediately to bring back their women and children, Hancock pronounced the council ended.[2]

Although the chiefs and warriors obediently rode away in the direction their women and children had taken, they did not bring them back. Nor did they return. Hancock waited, his anger rising, for a day or two. Then after ordering Custer to go after the Indians, he moved his troops into the abandoned camp. A list was made of all the lodges and their contents, then everything was promptly burned—251 tepees, 962 buffalo robes, 436 saddles, and hundreds of articles for cooking, eating, and living. The soldiers destroyed everything the Indians owned except the ponies they were riding and the blankets and clothing on their backs.

The frustration and rage of the Dog Soldiers, when they learned of the burning of their village, exploded across the plains. They raided stage stations, ripped out telegraph lines, and halted all travel along the Smoky Hill road. The war that Hancock had come to prevent, he had now foolishly caused. Custer galloped his 7th Cavalry from fort to fort, but found no Indians.

Many United States officials disapproved of the way Hancock had dealt with the Cheyennes. John B. Sanborn, who had been a member of many treaty commissions, wrote a strongly worded report to the Secretary of the Interior:

> The operations of General Hancock have been so disastrous to the public interests, and at the same time seem to me to be so inhuman, that I deem it proper to communicate my views to you on the subject. . . . For a mighty nation like us to be carrying on a war with a few straggling nomads, under such circumstances, is a spectacle most humiliating, an injustice unparalleled, a national crime most revolting, that must, sooner or later, bring down upon us or our posterity the judgment of Heaven.[3]

The war was, in any case, impractical and costly for the United States, and higher government authorities were eager to put an end to it. Hancock was recalled from the plains and in the summer of 1867 a new peace commission was formed.

The new peace plan for the southern plains included not only the Cheyennes and Arapahos, but the Kiowas, Comanches and Prairie Apaches. All five tribes would be moved to one great reservation south of the Arkansas River, given cattle herds, and taught how to grow crops.

Medicine Lodge Creek, south of Fort Larned, was chosen for the council; the meetings began in the Moon of the Changing Season, October 16. Although more than four thousand Indians were gathered at Medicine Lodge, few of the Dog Soldier Cheyennes participated. Since meeting General Hancock and his soldiers they had come to distrust peace meetings. Roman Nose and his followers were camped some sixty miles away; they were watching the council and would come in only if it pleased them. This worried the commissioners, who wanted to make peace with the hostile Dog Soldiers by convincing them that they would be better off living on the proposed reservation below the Arkansas.

The Kiowas and Comanches signed the treaty on October 21, but neither Black Kettle nor Little Raven and the Arapahos would agree to the terms until more Cheyennes came to Medicine Lodge. They were unwilling to sign the white men's treaties and risk losing the loyalty of the younger warriors in their tribes as they had after Sand Creek. The frustrated commissioners agreed to wait another week.

At last, on October 27, the Cheyenne chiefs and five hundred warriors came galloping up to the council grounds. As one of the Cheyennes sounded a bugle call, the ponies leaped forward in a charge, five hundred voices shouting "Hiya hi-i-i-ya!" The Indians fired their guns into the air, slid off their ponies, and began laughing and shaking hands with the startled commissioners. They had satisfactorily demonstrated the dash and bravery of the fighting Cheyennes.

The following morning, the Cheyenne and Arapaho chiefs

listened to a reading of the treaty, with George Bent inter-
preting. At first Bull Bear and White Horse refused to sign,
but Bent took them aside and convinced them it was the
only way to keep their power and live with the tribe. After
the signing, the commissioners gave out presents, including
ammunition for hunting. The Medicine Lodge council was
ended. Now most of the Cheyennes and Arapahos would
move south. But there were many others who would not go.
Three or four hundred were already heading north, their
fortunes cast with a warrior who would not surrender. The
name of Roman Nose was not signed to the treaty.

During the winter of 1867–68, most of the Cheyennes and
Arapahos were camped with Black Kettle below the Arkansas
near Fort Larned. From their autumn hunts they had enough
meat to survive the cold moons, but by spring the food shortage became serious. Although the Medicine Lodge treaty had
promised money to buy food and clothing and ammunition
to hunt buffalo, Tall Chief Wynkoop could give them few
supplies.

As the spring passed, the young men became increasingly
restless, grumbling because there was not enough to eat,
cursing the broken promises of the white men. In small bands
they began drifting northward to their old Smoky Hill hunting grounds. Tall Bull, White Horse, and Bull Bear gave in
to the demands of their proud Dog Soldiers, and also crossed
the Arkansas. Along the way, some of the wild young men
raided isolated settlements hoping to find food and guns.

Agent Wynkoop hurried to Black Kettle's village, begging
the chiefs to be patient and keep their young men off the
warpath.

"Our white brothers are pulling away from us the hand
they gave us at Medicine Lodge," Black Kettle said, "but
we will try to hold on to it. We hope the Great Father will take

pity on us and let us have the guns and ammunition he promised us so we can go hunt buffalo to keep our families from going hungry."[4]

Although Wynkoop was able to get a few obsolete rifles from General Philip Sheridan, the new Star Chief in Kansas, the Cheyennes and Arapahos who stayed to hunt below the Arkansas were very uneasy. Too many of their young men and most of the Dog Soldier bands were still north of the river. And some of them were raiding and killing white men wherever they could find them.

By late August most of the Cheyennes in the north were gathered along the Arikaree fork of the Republican River. Tall Bull, White Horse, and Roman Nose were there with about three hundred warriors and their families. A large band of Sioux was camped nearby. One day in the Moon When the Deer Paw the Earth, September 16, they learned that about fifty white men had been seen to the south. Only three or four of them wore blue uniforms; the others were dressed in rough frontier clothing. This was a special company organized by General Sheridan to search out Indian camps; they were known as Forsyth's Scouts.

The Cheyenne and Sioux chiefs agreed to join in an attack on the white scouts who had invaded their hunting grounds. Tall Bull and White Horse went to see Roman Nose, who was in his tepee undergoing purification ceremonies. A few days before, the Cheyennes had gone to feast with the Sioux. One of the Sioux women had used an iron fork to cook fried bread, and Roman Nose did not discover this until after he had eaten. Any metal touching his food was against his medicine. Roman Nose's magic power to escape the white men's bullets was worthless until he had purified himself. As soon as he was ready, he would come.

Riding their best war ponies and carrying their best lances, bows, and rifles, five or six hundred Sioux and Cheyenne

warriors moved south down the Arikaree Valley. The strategy was to attack the enemy all together as Roman Nose had
taught them. At daybreak, however, some of the rash young
braves tried to capture the white men's horse herd. This
alerted the Scouts and gave them time to move into good
defensive positions. For most of the morning the Indians
circled, unable to get through the fire of the Spencer repeating rifles.

Early in the afternoon Roman Nose arrived. He took a
position on high ground overlooking the action. Then an old
man, White Contrary, said: "Here is Roman Nose, the man
we depend upon, sitting behind this hill. All those people
fighting out there feel they belong to you, and they will do
all that you tell them, and here you are behind this hill."[5]

Roman Nose laughed. He had already made up his mind
what to do that day, and he knew he was going to die. He
went off to one side and prepared himself for battle, painting
his forehead yellow, his nose red, his chin black. Then he
put on his war bonnet with the forty feathers in its tail. When
he was ready, he rode to where the warriors were waiting
for him to lead them in a victorious charge.

They started out in a slow trot, then began to gallop. Once
again the rifle power of Forsyth's Scouts overpowered them.
As Roman Nose was caught in crossfire, a bullet penetrated
his spine.

For the young Cheyenne warriors, the death of Roman
Nose was like a great light going out in the sky. He had
believed and made them believe that if they would fight for
their country as Red Cloud was doing, they would someday
win.

Neither the Cheyennes nor the Sioux had any taste for
more fighting, but they kept Forsyth's Scouts trapped for
eight days until a relief column of soldiers arrived.

19. *White Horse, or Tsen-tainte.*
Photographed by William S. Soule
in 1870. Courtesy of the
Smithsonian Institution.

20. *Jacob Tall Bull. Photographed*
by DeLancey Gill, Washington
D.C., 1914. Courtesy of the
Smithsonian Institution.

21. *Little Robe. Photographer not*
recorded, but taken prior to 1877.
Courtesy of the Smithsonian
Institution.

22. *Yellow Bear. Photographed by*
John K. Hillers, 1875. Courtesy
of the Smithsonian
Institution.

After they had rested, many of the Cheyennes started moving south. With soldiers hunting for them everywhere now, their only hope of survival lay below the Arkansas, with their relatives. They looked upon Black Kettle as a beaten old man, but he was still alive, and he was chief of the Southern Cheyennes.

They had no way of knowing, of course, that Star Chief Sheridan was planning a winter campaign below the Arkansas. When the snows of the cold moons came, he would send Custer and his 7th Cavalry to destroy the villages of the "savage" Indians. To Sheridan, any Indian who resisted when shot at was a "savage."

That autumn, Black Kettle established a village on the Washita River. As the young men drifted back from the Smoky Hill country he scolded them for their wandering ways. But, like a forgiving father, he accepted them back into his band. Early in November, he heard rumors of soldiers coming. He traveled with three other chiefs almost a hundred miles to Fort Cobb, headquarters for the new Indian agency south of the Arkansas. They went to ask permission to move their lodges near there for protection. General William B. Hazen, the commander at Fort Cobb, refused to grant it. He assured Black Kettle that if his delegation would return to their villages and keep their young men there, they would not be attacked. After giving his visitors some sugar, coffee, and tobacco, Hazen sent them away, knowing he would probably never see any of them again. He was fully aware of Sheridan's war plans.

Facing into a raw north wind that turned into a snowstorm the disappointed chiefs made their way back to their villages, arriving on the night of November 26.

Black Kettle awoke just before dawn, as usual. He stepped outside his lodge, and was glad to see that the skies were clearing. A heavy fog hung over the Washita Valley, but he could see snow on the distant ridges.

Suddenly he heard the cries of a woman. Her voice became clearer as she came closer. "Soldiers! Soldiers!" she was shouting. Reacting automatically, Black Kettle rushed inside his lodge for his rifle. He had made up his mind to alert the camp and let everyone get away. He would meet the soldiers alone. There must not be another Sand Creek. As he shouted commands to everyone to mount and ride, his wife brought his pony to him.

Black Kettle expected the soldiers to come riding directly toward him, but instead they came dashing out of the fog from four directions. How could he meet four charging columns and talk to them of peace? It was Sand Creek all over again. He reached for his wife's hand, lifted her up behind him, and lashed the pony into motion. She had survived Sand Creek with him; now, like tortured dreamers dreaming the same nightmare over again, they were fleeing again from screaming bullets.

They were almost out of camp when he saw the charging soldiers in their heavy blue coats and fur caps. Black Kettle slowed his pony and lifted his hand in the sign gesture of peace. A bullet burned into his stomach, and his pony swerved. Another bullet caught him in the back, and he slid into the snow at the river's edge. Several bullets knocked his wife off beside him, and the pony ran away. The soldiers continued toward the camp, riding over Black Kettle and his wife, splattering mud upon their dead bodies.

Custer's orders from Sheridan were clearly stated: "to proceed . . . toward the Washita River, the supposed winter seat of the hostile tribes; to destroy their villages and ponies, to kill or hang all warriors, and bring back all women and children."[6]

In a matter of minutes Custer's troops destroyed Black

Kettle's village; in another few minutes of gory slaughter they destroyed several hundred corralled ponies. To kill or hang all the warriors meant separating them from the old men, women, and children. This proved too slow and dangerous for the soldiers; they found it more sensible to kill indiscriminately. They killed 103 Cheyennes, but only 11 of them were warriors. They captured 53 women and children.

By this time, gunfire had brought the Arapahos from their nearby village, and by about noontime, Kiowas and Comanches were arriving from farther downriver. When Custer saw the increasing number of warriors on the hills, he rounded up his troops and started back to his temporary camp north of the Washita River.

General Sheridan was there, eagerly waiting for news of a victory. When the troops marched in, waving the scalps of Black Kettle and the other dead "savages," Sheridan congratulated Custer for "efficient and gallant services rendered."

Tall Chief Wynkoop, who had already resigned in protest against Sheridan's policies, was far away in Philadelphia when he heard the news of Black Kettle's death. Wynkoop charged that his old friend had been betrayed and "met his death at the hands of white men in whom he had too often fatally trusted."[7]

Shortly after the Washita fight, Sheridan and Custer moved on to Fort Cobb, and from there sent runners to the four tribes in the area, warning them to come in and make peace or else be hunted down and killed.

The survivors of Black Kettle's band were the first to arrive at Fort Cobb. They had come on foot because Custer had killed all their ponies. A Cheyenne named Little Robe was acting as the leader of the tribe. Custer had burned their winter meat supply; they could find no buffalo along the Washita; they had eaten all their dogs. When Little Robe was taken to see Sheridan, he told the soldier chief that his people were starving.

Sheridan replied that the Cheyennes would be fed only if they all came into Fort Cobb and surrendered.

Little Robe knew there was only one answer to give. "It is for you to say what we have to do," he said.[8]

Yellow Bear of the Arapahos also agreed to bring his people to Fort Cobb. A few days later, Tosawi brought in the first band of Comanches to surrender. When he was taken to Sheridan, Tosawi's eyes brightened. He spoke his own name and added two words of broken English. "Tosawi, good Indian," he said.

It was then that General Sheridan replied, "The only good Indians I ever saw were dead."[9] These words were passed on by a lieutenant who was present and in time they became an American aphorism: *The only good Indian is a dead Indian.*

In the winter of 1868–69 some Dog Soldier bands had remained far north in their camps on the Republican; others under Tall Bull had come south for rations and protection.

During a move from Fort Cobb to a new reservation, Little Robe quarreled with Tall Bull, accusing him and his young men of causing much of the trouble with the soldiers. The Dog Soldier chief in turn accused Little Robe of being weak like Black Kettle and of bowing down before the white men. Tall Bull declared that he would not settle down on the poor reservation chosen for the Cheyennes below the Arkansas. He would take his people north and join the Northern Cheyennes, who with Red Cloud's Sioux had driven the white men from the Powder River country. The Cheyennes had always been a free people, he said. They should remain free or die.

And so, as they had done after Sand Creek, the Southern

branch of the tribe divided again. Almost two hundred Dog Soldier warriors and their families started north with Tall Bull. As they were preparing for the long and dangerous journey to the Powder River country, Sheridan sent a company of soldiers to search them out and destroy them.

To avoid the Bluecoats, Tall Bull and his people had to keep changing camps and moving about. They worked their way gradually westward across Nebraska into Colorado. It was July before Tall Bull could bring his band together for the final part of their journey—the crossing of the Platte. Because of high water in the river, they had to make camp.

By chance, that day some Pawnee scouts employed by the Bluecoats found the trail of the fleeing Cheyennes. With scarcely any warning, the Pawnees and the soldiers charged into Tall Bull's camp.

Many of the Cheyennes could not get away. Tall Bull and about twenty others took cover in a ravine. The Dog Soldier chief took his hatchet and cut footholds in the side of the ravine so that he could climb up to the top and fire at the attackers. He fired once, then ducked down, and when he rose to fire again, a bullet smashed his skull.

Roman Nose was dead; Black Kettle was dead; Tall Bull was dead. Now they were all good Indians. Like the antelope and the buffalo, the ranks of the proud Cheyennes were thinning to extinction.

8

Red Cloud's Visit to Washington

. . . today, by reason of the immense augmentation of the American population, and the extension of their settlements throughout the entire West, covering both slopes of the Rocky Mountains, the Indian races are more seriously threatened with a speedy extermination than ever before in the history of the country.

—DONEHOGAWA (ELY PARKER),
THE FIRST INDIAN COMMISSIONER OF INDIAN AFFAIRS

WHEN THE CHEYENNES who had not been killed with Tall Bull at last reached the Powder River country, they discovered that much had changed during the three winters they were in the South. Red Cloud had won his war and no more Bluecoats came north of the Platte. But there was confusion about the treaty Red Cloud had signed in 1868. He believed it was written that Fort Laramie was to be the Teton Sioux trading post. But the Bluecoats were now saying he had to move his people three hundred miles east to Fort Randall, on the Missouri River, where wild game was very scarce.

Spotted Tail had also been told that if he wanted supplies he would have to move to Fort Randall. And so he led his peaceful Brulés across the plains and settled there. But Red

Cloud would not go. He had won the Powder River country in a hard fight and Fort Laramie was the nearest trading post.

During the autumn of 1869 Indians everywhere on the Plains were at peace. It was said that the Great Father in Washington, President Grant, had chosen an Iroquois to be the Commissioner of Indian Affairs. This was Ely Parker, whose real name was Donehogawa, Keeper of the Western Door of the Long House of the Iroquois.

Then in the Moon When the Snow Drifts into the Tepees (January 1870) an ugly rumor came from the country of the Blackfeet in Montana. Soldiers had surrounded a camp of Piegan Blackfeet and killed them like trapped rabbits. These mountain Indians were old enemies of the Plains tribes, but everything was changing now. When soldiers killed Indians anywhere it made all the tribes uneasy. In many agencies Indians showed their anger by holding meetings and calling the Great Father "a fool and dog, without ears or brains." At two agencies buildings were set on fire and agents were held as prisoners.[1]

Commissioner Parker (or Donehogawa) believed that a general war would probably begin during the summer unless the government regained the Indians' trust. The commissioner knew about Red Cloud's unhappiness and his desire for a trading post near the Powder River country. Although Spotted Tail had gone to Fort Randall on the Missouri River, the Brulés were not happy there and had become rebellious. The commissioner decided to invite Red Cloud and Spotted Tail to Washington. If he could only win the confidence of these two Sioux chiefs, all the Plains Indians who followed them might be peaceful once more.

Red Cloud liked the idea of such a journey. It would give him a chance to talk to the Great Father and tell him the Sioux did not want a reservation on the Missouri. He could

23. *Ely Parker, or Donehogawa, Seneca chief, military secretary to U.S. Grant and Commissioner of Indian Affairs. Photographed around 1867. Courtesy of the Smithsonian Institution.*

also see for himself the commissioner named Parker who
was an Indian and could write like a white man.

On May 26, Red Cloud and fifteen Oglalas boarded a
special coach on the Union Pacific and started the long
journey east. It was a great experience, riding on their old
enemy, the Iron Horse. Chicago (a city named for Indians)
was terrifying with its noise and confusion and buildings that
seemed to reach the sky. The white men were as thick and
aimless as grasshoppers, moving always in a hurry but never
seeming to get anywhere.

After five days of clatter and motion, the Iron Horse
brought them into Washington. Commissioner Parker, who
truly was an Indian, greeted them warmly and asked Red
Cloud to speak for himself and his people.

"I have but a few words to say," Red Cloud responded.
"When I heard that my Great Father would permit me to
come to see him I was glad, and came right off. Telegraph
to my people, and say that I am safe. That is all I have to
say today."[2]

When Red Cloud and the Oglalas arrived at their hotel,
they were surprised to find Spotted Tail and a delegation of
Brulés waiting for them. Because Spotted Tail had obeyed
the government and moved his people to the Missouri River
agency, Commissioner Parker thought there might be trouble
between the two Teton chiefs. But when Spotted Tail told
Red Cloud that he and his Brulés hated the reservation and
wanted to return to their Nebraska hunting grounds, the
Oglala accepted the Brulé as a returned ally.

The next day, Donehogawa of the Iroquois took his guests
on a tour of the capital. For their journey, the Sioux had been
given white man's clothing, and it was obvious that most of
them were uncomfortable in their tight-fitting coats and but-
ton shoes. When Donehogawa told them that they were to

have their photographs taken, Red Cloud refused. "I am not a white man, but a Sioux," he explained. "I am not dressed for such an occasion."[3]

Donehogawa understood immediately and let his visitors know that if it pleased them they could dress in buckskins and moccasins for dinner with President Grant.

At the White House the Sioux were more impressed by the hundreds of blazing candles in chandeliers than they were by the invitation from the Great Father and by all the important men who had come to meet them. Spotted Tail, who enjoyed good food, especially liked the strawberries and ice cream. "Surely the white men have many more good things to eat than they send to the Indians," he said.

During the next few days, Donehogawa set about bargaining with Red Cloud and Spotted Tail. To make peace, he had to balance what they wanted against the political pressure of all the white men who were trying to get Indian land. He arranged for representatives from the different branches of government to meet with the Sioux visitors.

Red Cloud shook hands with Secretary of the Interior Jacob Cox and then stated his position clearly. "I do not want my reservation on the Missouri; this is the fourth time I have said so." He stopped for a moment, and gestured toward Spotted Tail and the Brulés. "Here are some people from there now. Their children are dying off like sheep; the country does not suit them. I was born at the forks of the Platte and I was told that the land belonged to me from north, south, east, and west. . . . [Then] they held a paper for me to sign, and that is all I got for my land. I know the people you send out there are liars. Look at me. I am poor and naked. I do not want war with my government. . . . I want you to tell all this to my Great Father."

Donehogawa of the Iroquois, the commissioner, replied:

"We will tell the President what Red Cloud has said today. The President told me he would talk with Red Cloud very soon."[4]

On June 9 when Grant met with the Sioux, Red Cloud repeated what he'd said earlier, emphasizing that his people did not want to live on the Missouri River. The treaty of 1868, he added, gave them the right to trade at Fort Laramie and have an agency on the Platte. Grant avoided a direct reply. He knew that the treaty, as it had been ratified by Congress, contained nothing about Fort Laramie or the Platte; it stated that the Sioux agency was to be "at some place on the Missouri." Privately Grant told Secretary of the Interior Cox and Commissioner Parker to call the Indians together the next day. The actual terms of the treaty had to be explained to them.

Donehogawa did not sleep well that night; he knew the Sioux had been tricked. When the printed treaty was read to them they would not like what they heard.

Next morning, after Secretary Cox went through the treaty point by point, Red Cloud said firmly: "This is the first time I have heard of such a treaty. I never heard of it and do not mean to follow it."

Secretary Cox replied that he did not believe any of the peace commissioners at Laramie would have told a lie about the treaty.

"I did not say the commissioners lied," Red Cloud answered, "but the interpreters were wrong. When the soldiers left the forts, I signed a treaty of peace, but it was not this treaty."

That night in their hotel the Sioux talked of going home the next day. Some said they were ashamed to tell their people how they had been lied to and cheated into signing the treaty of 1868. It would be better to die there in Washington. But Donehogawa persuaded them to come back for one more meeting. He promised to help them interpret the treaty in a better way. He had seen President Grant and convinced him that there was a solution to the difficulty.

This time, Secretary Cox explained that Red Cloud and his people had misunderstood. Although the Powder River country was *outside* the permanent reservation, it was *inside* the part set aside for hunting grounds. If some of the Sioux wanted to live on their hunting grounds instead of the reservation, they could. Nor would they have to go all the way to Fort Randall on the reservation to trade and receive their goods.

And so for the second time in two years, Red Cloud won a victory over the United States government, but this time he had the help of an Iroquois. He came forward and shook the commissioner's hand. "Yesterday, when I saw the treaty and all the false things in it," he said, "I was mad, and I suppose it made you the same. . . . Now I am pleased. . . . We have thirty-two nations and have a council house, just the same as you have. We held a council before we came here, and the demand I have made upon you is from the chiefs I left behind. We are all alike."

Secretary Cox, all smiles now, told Red Cloud that the government had planned a visit for the Sioux in New York on their way home.

"I do not want to go that way," Red Cloud replied. "I have seen enough of towns. . . . I have no business in New York. I want to go back the way I came. The whites are the same everywhere. I see them every day."[5]

Later, when he learned that he had been invited to make a speech to the people of New York, Red Cloud changed his mind. He was astonished by the warm acceptance that the audience gave him. For the first time he had the chance to talk to people instead of government officials.

"We want to keep peace," he told them. "Will you help us? In 1868 men came out and brought papers. We could not read them, and they did not tell us truly what was in them. . . . When I reached Washington the Great Father explained to me what the treaty was, and showed me that the interpreters had deceived me. All I want is right and just. I have tried to get from the Great Father what is right and just. I have not altogether succeeded."[6]

Red Cloud indeed had not altogether succeeded in getting what he believed was right and just. Although he returned to Fort Laramie with the good feeling that he had many white friends in the East, he found many white enemies waiting for him in the West. Land seekers, ranchers, and settlers were against a Sioux agency anywhere near the rich Platte valley and they had a great deal of political power in Washington.

Through the summer and autumn of 1870, Red Cloud and his lieutenant, Man-Afraid-of-His-Horses, worked hard for peace. At the request of Donehogawa they brought dozens of powerful chiefs into Fort Laramie for a council that was supposed to decide the location of the Sioux agency. Sitting Bull of the Hunkpapas was one of the few who would not come. "The white people have put bad medicine over Red Cloud's eyes," he said, "to make him see everything and anything they please."[7]

But Sitting Bull was wrong about Red Cloud. When the Oglala leader discovered that the government wanted to put the Sioux agency forty miles north of the Platte, he told white officials that he would have none of it. Confident that Donehogawa would support his refusal, Red Cloud then went off to the Powder River country for the winter.

Although his stubborn determination did win the Sioux a temporary agency on the Platte, they were permitted to use it for less than two years. By that time Donehogawa's political enemies had forced him to resign his position as Commissioner of Indian Affairs. In 1873 the Sioux agency was moved to the White River in Nebraska, out of the way of white immigration. Spotted Tail and his Brulés were also transferred to the same area. Within a year or so, Camp Robinson was established nearby. From this point on, the two Sioux tribes would be watched over and controlled by the Army.

9

The War for the Black Hills

No white person or persons shall be permitted to settle upon or occupy any portion of the territory, or without the consent of the Indians to pass through the same.
                                                    —Treaty of 1868

One does not sell the earth upon which the people walk.
                          —Tashunka Witko (Crazy Horse)

Not long after Red Cloud and Spotted Tail and their people settled down on their reservations in Nebraska, some white men discovered that gold was hidden in the Black Hills. Paha-Sapa, the Black Hills, was the center of the world, the place of gods and holy mountains, where warriors went to speak with the Great Spirit. The hills were sacred to the Indians. When they found white miners prospecting there, they killed them or chased them out.

In 1874, during the Moon of Red Cherries, the United States government sent more than a thousand soldiers to invade the Black Hills and protect the gold-hungry Americans, even though the treaty Red Cloud had signed in 1868 had given the Sioux this land forever and forbidden white men to enter it without permission. The soldiers were led by General George Armstrong Custer, the same Star Chief who had slaughtered Black Kettle's Cheyennes on the Washita six years earlier. The Sioux called him Pahuska, the Long Hair.

The young braves who returned to the Red Cloud agency after a summer of camping and hunting near the Black Hills were angry about Custer's invasion. When they went to Red Cloud with their complaints, he just told them to be patient. Like many other older chiefs, he had become so involved with the details of reservation life that he was losing touch with the younger tribesmen.

On October 22 a band of warriors decided to take action themselves and cut up a pine tree that the agency workmen were going to use for a flagpole. Custer had flown flags in his camps across the Black Hills; the Indians wanted no flags in their agency to remind them of soldiers.

The reservation agent immediately sent to the Soldiers' Town (Fort Robinson) for a company of pony soldiers. When the warriors saw the Bluecoats coming they fired their guns into the air and yelled war cries. Finally a band of agency Sioux arrived; they formed a ring around the pony soldiers and took them safely back to the agency stockade.

Again Red Cloud refused to interfere. When many of the protesting warriors started back north to spend the winter off the reservation, he apparently did not realize he was losing them forever. They had rejected his leadership for that of Sitting Bull and Crazy Horse, neither of whom had ever lived on a reservation or taken the white man's handouts.

By the spring of 1875, tales of Black Hills gold had brought hundreds of miners into this territory. The Army did remove a few, but no legal action was taken against them and they soon returned to prospect their claims.

At last alarmed by the white man's gold craze and the Army's failure to protect the Black Hills, Red Cloud and Spotted Tail protested to Washington officials. The Great Father's response was to send a commission "to treat with the

Sioux Indians for relinquishment of the Black Hills." In other words, the time had come to take away one more piece of territory that had been assigned to the Indians forever.

If the commissioners expected to meet quietly with a few chiefs to arrange an inexpensive trade, they were in for a surprise. When they arrived at the meeting place between the Red Cloud and Spotted Tail agencies, the plains for miles around were covered with Indian camps and herds of grazing cattle. All the nations of the Sioux and many of their Cheyenne and Arapaho friends had gathered there—more than twenty thousand Indians.

Few of them had ever seen a copy of the treaty of 1868 but they knew it said that before any part of the land it covered could be sold, three-fourths of all adult male Indians had to sign a new treaty. This knowledge gave them power; the commissioners faced thousands of angry, well-armed warriors.

Seeing the mood of the Indians, the commissioners realized the impossibility of trying to buy the Black Hills. They decided instead to bargain for the mineral rights. The Indians asked for time to hold their own meetings to consider all proposals about their land.

When the council met again on September 23, a commotion broke out just as Red Cloud was about to address the commissioners. About three hundred Oglalas from the Powder River country rode their ponies down a slope, occasionally firing off rifles. Some were chanting a song in Sioux:

> The Black Hills is my land and I love it
> And whoever interferes
> Will hear this gun.[1]

An Indian on a gray horse forced his way through to the central meeting point. He was Crazy Horse's messenger, Little Big Man, stripped for battle and wearing two revolvers belted to his waist. "I will kill the first chief who speaks for selling the Black Hills!" he shouted.[2]

The chiefs and commissioners must have guessed that Little Big Man expressed the feelings of most of the warriors present. And indeed, Spotted Tail finally spoke for the Sioux and made it clear that the Black Hills were not for rent or sale at any price.

The commissioners went back to Washington and recommended that Congress ignore the wishes of the Indians and fix a sum "as a fair equivalent of the value of the hills." This forced purchase of the Black Hills should be "presented to the Indians as a finality," they said.[3]

The government realized that the Indians would not give up the Black Hills without a fight. It was decided, therefore, to hunt down all the bands that still roamed freely there and put them on reservations. The reasoning was that once these "uncivilized" Indians were on reservations, all the mineral wealth of their territory could be seized by white citizens. Sioux and Cheyenne agents were told to notify all Indians off reservations to come in before January 31, 1876, or a "military force would be sent to compel them."[4]

When runners went out late in December to warn the non-agency chiefs of this command, heavy snows covered the northern Plains. It would have been impossible to move women and children in time to make the deadline. Both Sitting Bull and Crazy Horse said that they would consider the order to come in, but could not do so until the winter ended. "It was very cold," a young Oglala remembered, "and many of our people and ponies would have died in the snow. Also, we were in our own country and were doing no harm."[5]

The January 31 deadline was an excuse to make war against the independent Indians, and many of them accepted

24. *Little Big Man. Photo from the U.S. Signal Corps.*

it as that. But they never expected the Bluecoats to strike
so soon.

The first attack against the Indians came without warning
at dawn on March 17. A band of Northern Cheyennes and
Oglala Sioux had left Red Cloud agency for the Powder River
country, where they hoped to find a few buffalo and antelope. Fearing nothing in their own land, they were asleep
when three troops of cavalry began shooting into their camp.

The warriors immediately took up their weapons and tried
to hold the soldiers off until the women and children could
escape. "From a distance we saw the destruction of our village," Wooden Leg said. "Our tepees were burned with
everything in them. . . . I had nothing left but the clothing I
had on."[6]

When the battle ended, the chiefs led their homeless people toward Crazy Horse's camp, miles away to the northeast,
hoping to find food and shelter. The journey took three days,
the temperature was below zero at night, and there was very
little food.

Crazy Horse received them warmly and found room for
them in the Oglala tepees. "I'm glad you are come," he said
to a Cheyenne leader called Two Moon. "We are going to
fight the white man again."

"All right," Two Moon replied. "I am ready to fight. I have
fought already. My people have been killed, my horses
stolen; I am satisfied to fight."[7]

In the Geese Laying Moon, when the grass was tall and
the horses strong, Crazy Horse led the Oglalas and Cheyennes north to the Tongue River, where Sitting Bull and the
Hunkpapas had been living through the winter. Not long
after that, Lame Deer arrived with a band of Minneconjous
and asked to camp nearby.

As the weather got warmer, the tribes began moving north
in search of wild game and fresh grass for their horses. Along

the way they were joined by bands of Brulés, San Arcs, Blackfoot Sioux, and more Cheyennes. Most of them had left their reservations to hunt as their treaties permitted. They had all heard about the Bluecoats marching through the Sioux hunting grounds and wanted to be near Sitting Bull's powerful band of Hunkpapas in case there was trouble.

Early in June while they were camped along the Rosebud, the Hunkpapas had their yearly sun dance. For three days Sitting Bull danced, bled himself, and stared at the sun until he fell into a trance. When he rose again, he spoke to his people. In his vision he had heard a voice crying: "I give you these because they have no ears." Soldiers were falling from the sky like grasshoppers right into the Indian camp. Because the white men had no ears and would not listen, Wakantanka, the Great Spirit, was giving these soldiers to the Indians to be killed.[8]

A few days later a hunting party saw a column of Bluecoats led by General George Crook. These Plains Indians called him Three Stars instead of Gray Wolf. The hunters rode back to camp, sounding the cry of danger. It was decided that about a thousand warriors would travel through the night and attack Three Stars' soldiers. Sitting Bull, Crazy Horse, and Two Moon were among the leaders.

For a long time Crazy Horse had been waiting for a chance to test himself in battle with the Bluecoats. In all the years since the Fetterman fight at Fort Phil Kearny, he had been studying their ways of fighting. Each time he went into the Black Hills to seek visions, he had asked Wakantanka to give him secret powers so he could lead the Oglalas to victory. Since the time of his youth, Crazy Horse had known that the world men lived in was only a shadow of the real world. To get into the real world, he had to dream. If he could dream himself into the real world before a fight, he could endure everything.

On this day, June 17, 1876, Crazy Horse dreamed himself into the real world, and he showed the Sioux how to do many things they had never done before while fighting the white man's soldiers. He showed them how to strike at weak places in the enemy's lines and how to keep moving from one place to another. By midday he had confused the soldiers in three separate fights. By charging again and again on their fast ponies, the Sioux kept the soldiers apart and on the defensive.

When the sun went down, the fighting ended. The Indians knew they had given Three Stars a good fight, but they did not know until the next morning that they had whipped him. General Crook had to return to his base camp to wait for reinforcements. The Indians on the Rosebud were too strong for one column of soldiers.

After the fight on the Rosebud, the chiefs decided to move west to the valley of the Little Bighorn. Scouts had arrived with reports of great herds of antelope. They said there was much grass for the horses. No one knew for sure how many Indians spread their camps next to the river but it could not have been less than ten thousand people, including three or four thousand warriors. "It was a very big village and you could hardly count the tepees," Black Elk said.[9]

It was early in the Moon When the Chokecherries Are Ripe, with days hot enough for boys to swim in the melted snow water of the Little Bighorn. Hunting parties were coming and going to the mountains where a few buffalo as well as antelope had been found. During these peaceful times the chiefs of the different tribes met together in council. According to Wooden Leg, "There was only one who was considered as being above all the others. This was Sitting Bull. He was recognized as the one old man chief of all the camps combined."[10]

Sitting Bull did not believe the victory on the Rosebud had fulfilled his vision of soldiers falling into the Indian camp.

Since the retreat of Three Stars, however, no Bluecoats had been seen between the Powder and the Bighorn. The Indians did not know until the morning of June 24 that Long Hair Custer and his soldiers were marching toward the Indian camp.

Pte-San-Waste-Win, a cousin of Sitting Bull, was one of a group of young women digging wild turnips. She said the soldiers were six to eight miles away when first sighted. "We could see the flashing of their sabers and saw that there were very many soldiers in the party." These Indians were not aware of another attack, led by Major Marcus Reno, until they heard rifle fire from the direction of the Blackfoot Sioux lodges. "Like that, the soldiers were upon us. Through the tepee poles their bullets rattled. . . . We could still see the soldiers of Long Hair marching along in the distance, and our men, taken by surprise, and from a point whence they had not expected to be attacked, went singing the song of battle into the fight behind the Blackfoot village."[11]

Black Elk, a thirteen-year-old Oglala boy, was swimming with his friends in the Little Bighorn when he heard shouting in the Hunkpapa camp: "The chargers are coming! They are charging! The chargers are coming!" The warning was repeated by an Oglala crier and Black Elk could hear the cry going from camp to camp northward to the Cheyennes.[12]

When Two Moon received the warning, he ordered the Cheyenne warriors to their horses, and then told the women to take cover away from the tepee village. "I rode swiftly toward Sitting Bull's camp. Then I saw the white soldiers [Reno's men] fighting in a line. Indians covered the flat. They began to drive the soldiers all mixed up—Sioux, then soldiers, then more Sioux, and all shooting. The air was full of smoke and dust. I saw the soldiers fall back and drop into the riverbed like buffalo fleeing."[13]

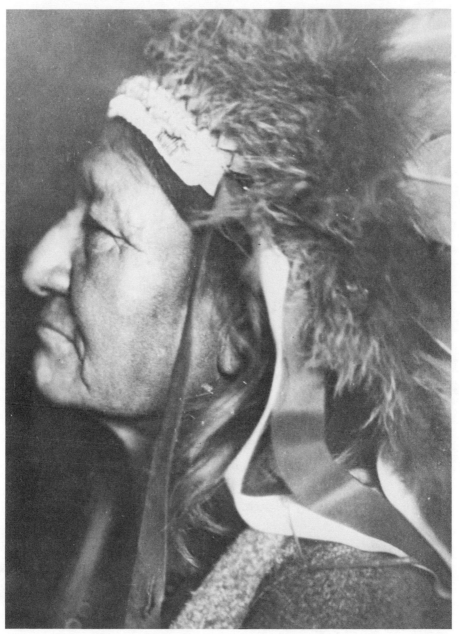

25. *Two Moon, chief of the Cheyennes. Courtesy of
Denver Public Library.*

The war chief who rallied the Indians and turned back
Reno's attack was a muscular, thirty-six-year-old Hunkpapa
named Gall. He had grown up in the tribe as an orphan.
Because of his skills as a hunter and warrior, Sitting Bull had
adopted him as a younger brother. By the summer of 1876
he was generally accepted by the Hunkpapas as Sitting Bull's
lieutenant, the war chief of the tribe.

Although Reno's men had been forced to retreat, Gall led
his warriors into the battle against Custer's column. Crazy
Horse and Two Moon were attacking also. Kill Eagle, a
Blackfoot Sioux chief, later said that the movement of Indians toward Custer's column was "like a hurricane . . . like
bees swarming out of a hive." The first massive charge caused
Custer and his men to become confused. Crow King, who
was with the Hunkpapas, said: "The greater portion of our
warriors came together in their front and we rushed our
horses on them. At the same time warriors rode out on each
side of them and circled around them until they were surrounded."[14]

Pte-San-Waste-Win watched at first from a distance. "The
smoke of the shooting and the dust of the horses shut out the
hill, and the soldiers fired many shots, but the Sioux shot
straight and the soldiers fell dead. The women crossed the
river after the men of our village, and when we came to the
hill there were no soldiers living and Long Hair lay dead
among the rest. . . . The blood of the people was hot and
their hearts bad, and they took no prisoners that day."[15]

Most Indians who told of the battle said they never saw
Custer and did not know who killed him. In an interview
given in Canada a year later, Sitting Bull said, "He did not
wear his long hair as he used to wear it. It was short, but it
was the color of the grass when the frost comes. . . . Where
the last stand was made, the Long Hair stood like a sheaf of

26. *Soldiers approaching village. From the pictographic account
of the Battle of the Little Bighorn drawn by Red Horse at
Cheyenne River Agency, South Dakota, in 1881.
Courtesy of the Smithsonian Institution.*

corn with all the ears fallen around him."[16] But Sitting Bull did not say who killed Custer.

The following day warriors were fighting some of Reno's men farther down the river when warnings came of many more soldiers marching in the direction of the Little Bighorn.

After a council it was decided to break camp. The warriors had used up most of their ammunition and they knew it would be foolish to try to fight with bows and arrows alone. The women were told to begin packing, and before sunset they started up the valley toward the Bighorn Mountains. Along the way the tribes separated and took different directions.

When the white men in the East heard of the Long Hair's defeat, they called it a massacre and went crazy with anger. Because they could not punish Sitting Bull and the war chiefs, the Great Council in Washington decided to punish the Indians they could find—those who remained on the reservations and had not been involved in the fighting.

On July 22 the Great Warrior Sherman took military control of all the reservations in the Sioux country and began to treat the Indians there as prisoners of war. On August 15 the Great Council made a new law requiring the Indians to give up all rights to the Powder River country and the Black Hills. They did this without regard to the treaty of 1868, claiming that the Indians had broken the treaty by going to war with the United States. The reservation Indians found this difficult to understand. They had not attacked United States soldiers, nor had Sitting Bull's followers attacked them until Custer sent Reno charging through the Sioux villages.

Then in September the Great Father sent a new commission to give the reservation Indians legal papers transferring the vast wealth of the Black Hills to white ownership. Bishop

27. *Major Reno's column turned and retreating. From the pictographic account of the Battle of the Little Bighorn drawn by Red Horse at Cheyenne River Agency, South Dakota, in 1881. Courtesy of the Smithsonian Institution.*

Henry Whipple, a member of the commission, tried to explain the papers in language that could be used by interpreters.

> When the Great Council made the appropriation this year to continue your supplies they made certain provisions, three in number, and unless they were complied with no more appropriations would be made by Congress. Those three provisions are: first, that you shall give up the Black Hills country and the country to the north; second, that you shall receive your rations on the Missouri River; and third, that the Great Father shall be permitted to locate three roads from the Missouri River across the reservation to that new country where the Black Hills are.[17]

Most of the chiefs knew it was already too late to save the Black Hills, but they protested strongly against having their reservations moved to the Missouri. "I think if my people should move there," Red Cloud said, "they would all be destroyed. There are a great many bad men there and bad whiskey; therefore I don't want to go there."[18]

Spotted Tail accused the government and the commissioners of betraying the Indians, of broken promises and false words. "This war did not spring up here in our land; this war was brought upon us by the children of the Great Father who came to take our land from us without price, and who, in our land, do a great many evil things. . . . This war has come from robbery—from the stealing of our land."[19] Spotted Tail was against moving to Missouri. And he told the commissioners he would not sign away the Black Hills until he could go to Washington and talk to the Great Father.

The commissioners gave the Indians a week to talk over the terms. But it soon became clear that they were not going to sign. To break down their opposition, the commission hinted that if they didn't agree to the terms of the papers, the Great Council in its anger would cut off all rations immediately, would move them to Indian Territory in the South and take away all their guns and horses.

Now there was no way out for the Indians. The Black Hills were stolen; the Powder River country and its herds of wild game were gone. Without wild game or rations, the people would starve. The thought of moving far away to a strange country in the South was unbearable. Further, if their horses and guns were taken away they would no longer be men.

At last Red Cloud and Spotted Tail and their people signed. After that the commissioners went to the agencies of the other Sioux tribes and forced them to sign. Thus did Paha-Sapa, its spirits and its mysteries, its vast pine forests, and its billion dollars in gold come to be owned by the United States instead of by the Indians.

Four weeks later, soldiers marched out of Fort Robinson into the agency camps to take away the reservation Indians' ponies and guns and place all males under arrest. From this time on, the Sioux would have to live at Fort Robinson surrounded by soldiers. Red Cloud, Spotted Tail, and the others had sacrificed the Black Hills to keep what little freedom remained to them. Now that too had been taken away.

Meanwhile, the United States Army, in a search for revenge, was prowling the country north and west of the Black Hills, killing Indians wherever it found them. In late summer of 1876, some of Three Stars Crook's men came upon a village of Oglalas and Minneconjous. These Indians were led by a chief called American Horse and were moving south to spend the winter on their reservation. Most of them escaped when the soldiers attacked. But American Horse, four warriors, and fifteen women and children were trapped in a cave. Crook arrived later and ordered the soldiers to fire into the mouth of the cave. American Horse was badly wounded and many of the others were killed before surrendering.

Some of the Sioux who had escaped made their way to Sitting Bull's camp and told him about the attack. Sitting Bull and Gall with about six hundred warriors went to help American Horse but it was too late. All they could do was rescue the helpless survivors and bury the dead. "What have we done that the white people want us to stop?" Sitting Bull asked. "We have been running up and down this country, but they follow us from one place to another."[20]

By springtime of 1877, meeting soldiers all the way north along the Yellowstone, Sitting Bull grew tired of running. He decided there was no longer room enough in the Great Father's country for white men and the Sioux to live together. Because he did not intend ever to become an agency Indian, he decided to take his people to Canada, to the land of the Grandmother, Queen Victoria. Before he started, he searched for Crazy Horse, hoping to persuade him to bring the Oglalas to the Grandmother's land. But Crazy Horse's people were continually on the move trying to escape the soldiers, and Sitting Bull could not find them.

In those same cold moons, General Crook was also looking for Crazy Horse. This time Crook had put together a mighty army which swept through the Powder River country like a horde of grizzly bears, crushing all Indians in its path. Before the soldiers found Crazy Horse, they found a Cheyenne village first, Dull Knife's village. Most of these Cheyennes had not been in the Little Bighorn battle, but had slipped away from the Red Cloud agency in search of food after the Army had taken over and stopped their rations.

It was in the Deer-Rutting Moon, and very cold. The soldiers struck at dawn. They caught the Cheyennes in their lodges, killing them as they awoke. The warriors held off the soldiers for a while, then followed after their women and children to the Bighorns. They knew only one place of safety —Crazy Horse's village.

During the first night of the journey, twelve infants and several old people froze to death. The next night, the men killed some of the ponies, and thrust the small children into the carcasses to keep them from freezing. The old people put their hands and feet in beside the children. For three days they walked across the frozen snow, their bare feet leaving a trail of blood. At last they reached Crazy Horse's camp.

Crazy Horse shared food, blankets, and shelter with Dull Knife's people, but warned them to be ready to move. Crook's soldiers were coming at them from both the north and the south. To survive they would have to keep running.

All during the cold moons, Crazy Horse and his Oglalas held out. In February, they were camped near the Little Powder, living off what game they could find, when runners brought news that Spotted Tail and a party of Brulés were coming from the south. Three Stars Crook had promised Spotted Tail that the reservation Sioux would not have to move to the Missouri River if he could persuade Crazy Horse to surrender. This was the purpose of Spotted Tail's visit.

Just before the Brulés arrived, Crazy Horse told his father that he was going away. He asked his father to shake hands with Spotted Tail and tell him that the Oglalas would come in as soon as the weather was warmer. Then he went off into the Bighorns alone. Crazy Horse had not made up his mind yet whether he would surrender; perhaps he would let his people go while he stayed in the Powder River country— like an old Buffalo cast out of the herd. When Spotted Tail arrived, he guessed that Crazy Horse was avoiding him. Messengers went out to look for the Oglala leader, but he had vanished in the deep snows.

Crook next sent Red Cloud to find Crazy Horse and promise him a reservation in the Powder River country if he surrendered. Crazy Horse's nine hundred Oglalas were starving, his warriors had no ammunition, and their horses were thin and bony. The promise of a reservation in the Powder River country brought Crazy Horse to Fort Robinson to surrender.

The last of the Sioux war chiefs now became a reservation Indian with no authority over his people, a prisoner of the Army, which had never defeated him in battle. Yet, he was still a hero to the young men. Their admiration often caused jealousy among the older agency chiefs. Crazy Horse remained aloof; he and his followers lived only for the day when Three Stars would make good his promise of a reservation in the Powder River country.

Late in the summer of 1877, Crazy Horse heard that Three Stars wanted him to go to Washington to talk with the Great Father about the promised reservation. Crazy Horse refused. He had seen what happened to chiefs who went to the Great Father's house in Washington; they came back fat from the white man's way of living with all the hardness gone out of them. He could see the changes in Red Cloud and Spotted Tail, and they knew he saw and they did not like him for it.

In August news came that the Nez Percés, who lived beyond the Shining Mountains, were at war with the Bluecoats. Soldier chiefs began enlisting warriors to do their scouting for them against the Nez Percés. Crazy Horse told the young men not to go against those other Indians far away, but some would not listen, and allowed themselves to be bought by the soldiers. On August 31, the day these former Sioux warriors put on their Bluecoat uniforms to march away, Crazy Horse was so sick with disgust that he said he was going to take his people back north to the Powder River country.

When Three Stars heard of this from his spies, he ordered Crazy Horse arrested. Crazy Horse tried to get away but was taken back to Fort Robinson and turned over to a soldier chief and one of the agency policemen. Crazy Horse stared hard at the agency policeman. He was Little Big Man, who not so long ago had defied the commissioners who came to steal Paha-Sapa, the same Little Big Man who had threatened to kill the first chief who spoke for selling the Black Hills. Now the white men had bought Little Big Man and made him an agency policeman.

As Crazy Horse walked between them, letting the soldier chief and Little Big Man lead him away, he must have tried to dream himself into the real world, to escape the darkness of a shadow world in which all was madness. Soon they were standing in the doorway of a building. The windows were barred with iron, and he could see men behind the bars with chains on their legs. It was a trap for an animal and Crazy Horse lunged away like a trapped animal, with Little Big Man holding on to his arm. Someone shouted a command, and a soldier thrust a bayonet deep into Crazy Horse's stomach.

Crazy Horse died that night, September 5, 1877, at the age of thirty-five. All through the Moon of Drying Grass, mourners watched beside his burial place. And then in the Moon of Falling Leaves came the heartbreaking news: the reservation Sioux must leave Nebraska and go to a new reservation on the Missouri River in Dakota.

Through the crisp dry autumn of 1877, long lines of exiled Indians marched toward the barren land. Along the way, several bands slipped away and turned north, determined to escape to Canada and join Sitting Bull. With them went the father and mother of Crazy Horse, carrying the heart and bones of their son. At a place known only to them they buried Crazy Horse near Chankpe Opi Wakpala, the creek called Wounded Knee.

10

Cheyenne Exodus

All we ask is to be allowed to live, and live in peace. I seek no war with anyone. An old man, my fighting days are done.
—TAHMELAPASHME (DULL KNIFE)
OF THE NORTHERN CHEYENNES

IN THE MOON OF GREENING GRASS, 1877, when Crazy Horse came into Fort Robinson, many bands of Cheyennes who were with him during the winter also surrendered. Among the Cheyenne chiefs were Little Wolf, Dull Knife, and Standing Elk. Together their people numbered about one thousand.

These Cheyennes expected to live on the reservation with the Sioux as set down in the treaty of 1868, which Little Wolf and Dull Knife had signed. But agents from the Indian Bureau recommended that the Northern Cheyennes be sent to Indian Territory to live with their kinsmen, the Southern Cheyennes.

The country near the Black Hills was home to the Northern Cheyennes. For many years they had lived and fought with the Sioux. They did not want to go south.

Therefore, when orders came through from Washington for them to be taken to Indian Territory, the chiefs asked for a final council with Three Stars Crook. Crook tried to reassure them and said that if they did not like the Indian Territory they could come back north. (At least that was the way the interpreters translated Crook's words.)

The Army put Lieutenant Henry W. Lawton in charge of the Cheyennes on the long journey south. "He was a good man," Wooden Leg said, "always kind to the Indians."[1] They called Lawton the Tall White Man and were pleased when he let the old and sick people ride in the soldier wagons and gave them army tents to sleep in. The Tall White Man also saw that everyone had enough bread and meat and coffee and sugar.

On the way south, the Cheyennes discovered that the Plains were changing. There were railroads and fences and buildings everywhere now. They saw only a few small herds of buffalo and antelope. The Tall White Man gave rifles to thirty warriors chosen by the chiefs so they could go out and hunt.

On August 5, 1877, after more than three months of traveling, they reached Fort Reno on the Cheyenne-Arapaho reservation. A day or so later the Southern Cheyennes invited their northern relatives to a customary tribal feast for newcomers. It was there that Little Wolf and Dull Knife made their first sad discovery. The feast consisted of a pot of watery soup; this was all the Southerners had to offer. There was not enough to eat in this empty land—no wild game, no clear water to drink. The agents did not have enough food for all of them. To make matters worse, the summer heat was unbearable and the air was filled with mosquitoes and flying dust.

Little Wolf went to the agent, John D. Miles, and told him they had only come to look at the reservation. Now, because they did not like it, they were ready to go back north as Three Stars Crook had promised they could do. The agent answered that only the Great Father in Washington could decide whether the Northern Cheyennes could go back to the Black Hills country. He promised to get more food; a beef herd was being driven up from Texas for them.

The Texas longhorns were scrawny, and their meat was tough, but at least the Northern Cheyennes could now make soup as their relatives did. In late summer, the Northerners began to fall sick with malaria. "Our people died, died, died, kept following one another out of this world."[2]

At last the Army sent Lieutenant Lawton, the Tall White Man, to inspect the Northern Cheyenne camp. "They are not getting supplies enough to prevent starvation," Lawton reported. "Many of their women and children are sick for want of food. A few articles I saw given them they would not use themselves, but said they would take them to their children, who were crying for food. . . . The beef I saw given them was of very poor quality, and would not have been considered merchantable *for any use*."

The post doctor had no quinine to treat the malaria which had become an epidemic. "He frequently locked up his office because he had no medicines and went away, because he did not want to be called upon by the Indians when he could do nothing for them."[3]

The Tall White Man called the chiefs together, not to talk to them but to listen. "We came down on the word of General Crook," Dull Knife said. "We are still strangers in this country. We wish to get settled down where we are to live permanently and then we will send our children to school."

Other chiefs spoke up more strongly then and told of the sickness and death among the people. The Cheyennes had agreed to use the white man's medicine, but they could find no doctor who would give them any. If they could go hunting, they said, they could have buffalo meat to make them well again.

Not until the coming of the cold moons did agent Miles permit the Northern Cheyennes to go out for a buffalo hunt,

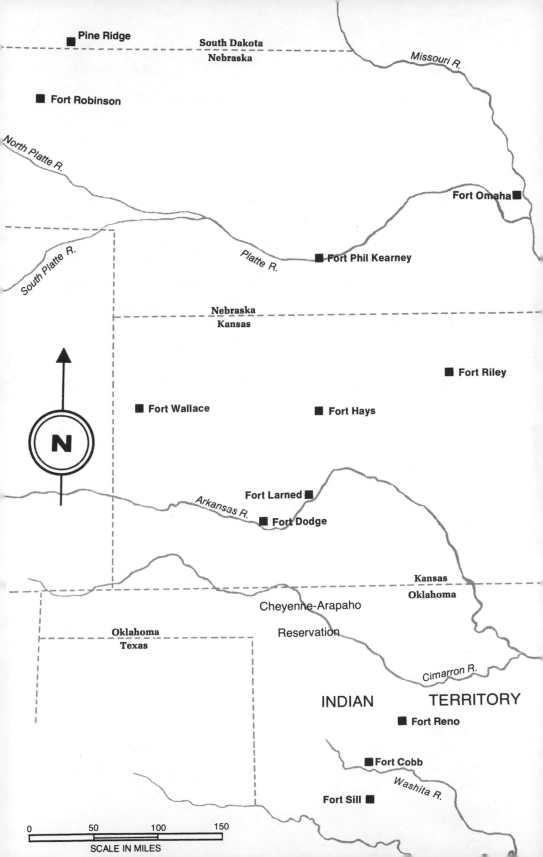

and then he put some of the Southerners to spy on them to make certain they would not run away to the north. The buffalo hunt was such a failure that the hunters would have joked about it if everyone hadn't been starving for meat. Ghostly heaps of buffalo bones left by white hunters were everywhere on the southern Plains but the Cheyennes could find nothing to hunt but a few coyotes. They killed the coyotes and ate them, and before the winter was over they had to eat all their dogs.

When the weather warmed up, mosquitoes began swarming in the reservation swamps, and soon the Northern Cheyennes again contracted malaria. To add to the illnesses, a measles epidemic struck the children. In the Moon of Red Cherries, there were so many burial ceremonies that the chiefs went to confront agent Miles. Little Wolf and Dull Knife were both getting old—well into their fifties—and they knew it did not matter very much what happened to them. But it was their duty to save the young people, the tribe itself, from being wiped off the earth.

At the meeting, Miles asked them to stay on for one more year. Little Wolf was the spokesman and he answered firmly, "We cannot stay another year; we want to go now. Before another year has passed, we may all be dead, and there will be none of us left to travel north."[4]

The chiefs realized that they would not be allowed to leave the reservation. They were divided as to what to do. Some were fearful of starting back north. The soldiers would track them down and kill them all; it was better to die on the reservation. But Little Wolf and Dull Knife were willing to take their chances. During the night of September 9, 1878, they told their people to pack and be ready to start at first daylight. They left their tepees and headed north—237 men, women, and children. Less than a third of them were warriors—the strongest of heart in a proud, doomed tribe. There were not enough horses, so they took turns riding and walking.

In the days when there were thousands of Cheyennes, they had more horses than any of the Plains tribes. They were called the Beautiful People then. Now, fate had turned against them both in the south and in the north.

For three days they traveled, driving their horses hard. The soldiers caught up with them 150 miles north of Fort Reno across the Cimarron River. The Cheyennes hid themselves well, however, and were able to keep the soldiers trapped for a day and a night in a place where four canyons crossed.

Now the fight became a running battle across Kansas and into Nebraska. Soldiers swarmed from all the forts along the way. To keep moving fast, the Cheyennes had to trade their horses for white men's. They tried to avoid fights, but ranchers, cowboys, and settlers all joined in the chase. Ten thousand soldiers and three thousand white men came after them. Still the Cheyennes kept moving north.

At one night camp after they had crossed the Platte, the chiefs took a count. Thirty-four of those who had started from Indian Territory were missing. Some had scattered during the fights and were making their way north by other trails. Most, however, had died from the white men's bullets. The older people were weak now, and the children had not had enough food or sleep. They could not travel much farther. Also, the cold moons would soon be upon them. Dull Knife suggested that the Cheyennes go to Red Cloud's agency and ask him for food and shelter. Many times they had helped Red Cloud when he was fighting for the Powder River country. Now it was his turn to help the Cheyennes.

Little Wolf scorned such talk. He was going to Cheyenne country, to the Tongue River valley, where they could find plenty of meat and live like Cheyennes again.

It was decided to split up. Those who wanted to go on to the Tongue River would follow Little Wolf. Those who were tired of running could follow Dull Knife to Red Cloud's agency. The next morning some hundred and fifty people went off with Dull Knife—a few warriors, the old, the children, and the wounded. In the end, Wild Hog and Left Hand decided to go as well. They wanted to stay with their children, the last strong seed of the Beautiful People.

On October 23, when Dull Knife's group was only two days from Fort Robinson, a group of soldiers surrounded them. When the captain in command learned that they were looking for Red Cloud, he told Dull Knife some disappointing news. During the months the Cheyennes had been in the south, both the Red Cloud and Spotted Tail agencies had been moved far north to Dakota. Fort Robinson was still open, however, and the soldiers offered to take them there.

At first Dull Knife objected. But an early snow had started to fall. The Cheyennes were already cold and hungry. Dull Knife said he would follow the soldiers to the fort.

That night the chiefs talked uneasily about what the soldiers might do with them. They decided to take apart their best guns and hide them. The women put the gun barrels under their clothing, and tied the pins, cartridges, and other small pieces to beads and moccasins as though they were ornaments. The next morning when the soldier chief ordered the Cheyennes to disarm, they made a small pile of only their old, broken guns and their bows and arrows.

On October 25 they reached Fort Robinson and were put in a log barracks that had been built for half their number. Although the Cheyennes were crowded, they were glad to have shelter at last. The soldier guards gave them blankets and food and medicine, and looked at them with friendliness and admiration.

Each day Dull Knife asked the post commander when they could go to Red Cloud's new agency. But no orders came from Washington about the move. To show his sympathy for the Cheyennes, the commander gave some warriors permission to go out and hunt wild game. Even though few animals were left and the prairie was empty and lonesome with all the tepees gone, the Cheyennes enjoyed the freedom to roam.

Then early in the Moon When the Wolves Run Together, a new post commander, Henry W. Wessells, arrived. Captain Wessells did not like or trust the Cheyennes; he was always coming into their barracks and spying on them. It was also during this moon that Red Cloud was brought down from Pine Ridge, his reservation in Dakota, to talk with them:

"Our hearts are sore for you," Red Cloud said. "Many of our blood are among your dead. This has made our hearts bad. But what can we do? The Great Father is all-powerful. His people fill the whole earth. We must do what he says. We have begged him to allow you to come to live among us. We hope he may let you come. What we have we will share with you. But remember, what he directs, that you must do. We cannot help you. The snows are thick on the hills. Our ponies are thin. The game is scarce. You cannot resist, nor can we. So listen to your old friend and do without complaint what the Great Father tells you."

So Red Cloud had become old and cautious in his later years. Dull Knife had heard he was a prisoner on his own Dakota reservation. The Cheyenne chief stood up, looking sadly at his old Sioux brother. "We know you for our friend, whose words we may believe," he said. ". . . We bowed to the will of the Great Father and went far into the south where he told us to go. There we found a Cheyenne cannot live. Sickness came among us that made mourning in every lodge.

Then the treaty promises were broken, and our rations were short. Those not worn by diseases were wasted by hunger. To stay there meant that all of us would die. Our petitions to the Great Father were unheeded. We thought it better to die fighting to regain our old homes than to perish of sickness. Then our march was begun. The rest you know."

Dull Knife then turned to Captain Wessells: "Tell the Great Father that Dull Knife and his people ask only to end their days here in the north where they were born. Tell him we want no more war. . . . Tell him if he lets us stay here Dull Knife's people will hurt no one. Tell him if he tries to send us back we will butcher each other with our own knives."[5]

But less than a month later, January 3, 1879, a message came from the War Department. General Sheridan had made up his mind about Dull Knife's Cheyennes. "Unless they are sent back to where they came from," Sheridan said, "the whole reservation system will receive a shock which will endanger its stability."[6]

The order was for an immediate move, in spite of the winter weather. It was the Moon When the Snow Drifts into the Tepees, the season of bitter cold and raging blizzards.

"Does the Great Father desire us to die?" Dull Knife asked Captain Wessells. "If so, we will die right here. We will not go back!"[7]

Wessells answered that he would give the Cheyennes five days to change their minds. During that time they would be kept prisoners and would get no food or wood for the heating stove.

And so for five days the Cheyennes huddled together in the barracks without anything to eat. Snow fell almost every night. They scraped it off the window ledges for drinking water.

On January 9 Wessells came to talk to them. "Let the women and children out," he ordered, "so they will no longer suffer."

"We'll all die here together sooner than be sent south," they answered.[8] After Wessells went away, one of the warriors lifted up a section of the floor. Below were five gun barrels, hidden there since they had first come to Fort Robinson. Then they began collecting triggers and hammers and cartridges from ornaments and moccasins. Soon they had reassembled rifles and a few pistols. The young men painted their faces and put on their best clothing. The women stacked up their possessions under each window to make it easier to leap out quickly.

At 9:45 in the evening, the first shots were fired and every window was smashed open. The Cheyennes poured from the building. They seized rifles from the guards they had wounded and ran toward the hills beyond the post. The first soldiers who rode after them were dressed only in their winter underwear. But more soldiers kept coming all the time, and they shot every Indian they saw moving across the snow. In the first hour of fighting, more than half the warriors died. Then the soldiers began chasing the scattered bands of women and children, killing many of them before they could surrender.

When morning came, the soldiers took the captured Cheyennes back to Fort Robinson. Thirty-eight managed to escape and were still alive and free. But several days later, thirty-two of them were trapped in a deep rut made by the buffalo herds. The soldiers stood at the edge of it, and emptied their guns over and over until no shooting was returned by the Indians. Of these, nine Indians survived and were taken captive.

The six remaining free Cheyennes, including Dull Knife

and his family, made their way north to Pine Ridge. There they became prisoners on Red Cloud's reservation.

Little Wolf and those who had chosen to go with him to the Tongue River country spent the winter hidden in pits dug along the bank of a small stream. When the weather warmed up, they started once more for Tongue River country. It was then that Little Wolf learned that Lieutenant William P. Clark was looking for him.

In the early days at Fort Robinson this soldier chief, whom the Cheyennes called White Hat, had been Little Wolf's friend. White Hat had given Little Wolf the chance to stay on at Fort Robinson, but he had chosen instead to go south with his people. Now, a year and a half later, the two men met again. White Hat disarmed himself to show he had confidence in their friendship. He said that his orders were to take the Cheyennes to Fort Keogh nearby, where some of their relatives were now living.

"Since I left you at Red Cloud agency," Little Wolf answered, "we have been down south, and have suffered a great deal down there. . . . You are the only one who has offered to talk before fighting, and it looks as though the wind, which has made our hearts flutter for so long, would now go down."[9]

After Little Wolf was sure that White Hat would not let the soldiers destroy his people, he gave up his guns. They went on to Fort Keogh and there most of the young men signed up as scouts. "For a long time we did not do much except to drill and work at getting out logs from the timber," Wooden Leg said. "I learned to drink whiskey at Fort Keogh. . . . I spent most of my scout pay for whiskey."[10] The Cheyennes drank whiskey from boredom and despair. It made the white traders rich and it destroyed what was left of the leadership of the tribe. It destroyed Little Wolf.

After months and months of waiting, the Cheyennes at Fort Keogh were given a reservation on Tongue River, and Dull Knife and the few left at Pine Ridge were allowed to join their people.

For most of them it was too late. The strength had gone out of the Cheyennes. In the years since Sand Creek, doom had stalked the Beautiful People. The seed of the tribe was scattered with the wind. Soon there would be no one left to recall the past, no one left to speak their names after they were gone.

11

Dance of the Ghosts

*If a man loses anything and goes back and looks carefully for it
he will find it, and that is what the Indians are doing now when
they ask you to give them the things that were promised them in
the past; and I do not consider that they should be treated like
beasts, and that is the reason I have grown up with the feelings
I have.*

—TATANKA YOTANKA (SITTING BULL)

*All Indians must dance, everywhere, keep on dancing. Pretty soon
in next spring Great Spirit come. He bring back all game of every
kind. The game be thick everywhere. All dead Indians come back
and live again. They all be strong just like young men, be young
again.*

—WOVOKA, THE PAIUTE MESSIAH

IN 1877 after the Sioux had surrendered the Black Hills and
were driven out of Nebraska, what they had left was a
shrunken area of Dakota land. The divisions of the Sioux were
given separate agencies on the new reservation. Red Cloud's
Oglalas settled at Pine Ridge; Spotted Tail and his Brulés
settled at the Rosebud. The other agencies were Lower
Brulé, Crow Creek, Cheyenne River, and Standing Rock.
Though the agencies have remained there for almost a century, most of the reservation land which separated them has
been gradually taken from the Indians.

As the Sioux were settling down on their new agencies, a great wave of immigration poured into Dakota. Settlers going west wanted roads. They also wanted a railroad built across the reservation. Businessmen who wanted cheap land to sell to immigrants thought up schemes to break up the Great Sioux Reservation.

In the old days the Sioux would have fought to keep all these white men out of their territory, but now they had no weapons. They could not even feed and clothe themselves. Their greatest living war leader, Sitting Bull, was an exile in Canada. But someday he and his three thousand followers might return.

For the United States government, Sitting Bull was a dangerous symbol of defiance. An army officer who tried unsuccessfully to bring Sitting Bull back to the United States wrote to the War Department: "The presence of this large body of Indians, bitterly hostile to us, in close proximity to the frontier, is a standing menace to the peace of our Indian territories."[1]

Sitting Bull's exiles might have stayed in Canada forever. But they were not welcome there. The Canadian government saw them as possible troublemakers and refused to help them in any way. Wild game was scarce and in the bitter winters the Indians suffered badly. "We began to feel homesick for our own country where we used to be happy," said one of the young Oglalas.[2] As the seasons passed, a few hungry and ragged families drifted south across the border to surrender at the Sioux agencies in Dakota.

Sitting Bull begged the Canadian government to give his people a reservation where they could support themselves. He was told that because he came from the United States he had no rights to land. During the bad winter of 1880, many Sioux horses froze to death; and when spring came more of the exiles began heading south on foot. Several of Sitting Bull's most loyal lieutenants, including Gall, gave up and went to the Great Sioux Reservation.

At last on July 19, 1881, Sitting Bull and 186 of his remaining followers crossed the border and rode into the nearest military fort. The Hunkpapa chief was wearing a calico shirt, a pair of shabby leggings, and a dirty blanket. He looked old and beaten when he surrendered his rifle to the commanding officer.

Sitting Bull was held as a military prisoner for almost two years before being transferred to the Hunkpapa agency at Standing Rock. But during this time Sioux chiefs and subchiefs from everywhere on the Great Reservation came to honor him. Newspapermen wanted interviews. Sitting Bull thought he had been forgotten. Instead, he was famous. In 1882 representatives from the different Sioux agencies came to ask his advice about a new government plan to break up the Great Sioux Reservation and sell about half the land for white settlement. Sitting Bull advised them not to sell; the Sioux had no land to spare.

Even though they did decide to keep their land, in 1882 the Sioux were almost tricked out of it. A United States commission traveled from one agency to another and told the Indians that if they signed some papers they would be given twenty-six thousand cattle. The Indians could not read, and they were never told that they were signing away fourteen thousand miles of territory in return for the promised cattle.

Fortunately for the Sioux, they had enough friends in Washington to question the commission's methods. They pointed out that even if the land had been given legally, the necessary three-fourths of all adult male Sioux had not signed the papers.

Another commission, headed by Senator Henry L. Dawes,

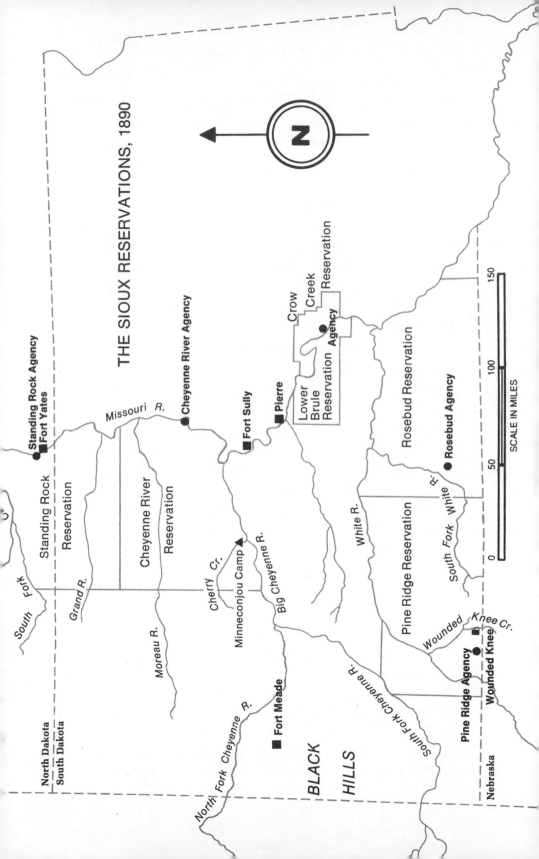

THE SIOUX RESERVATIONS, 1890

N

Standing Rock Agency
■ **Fort Yates**

● Standing Rock
Reservation

South Fork

Grand R.

Moreau R.

Cheyenne River
Reservation

Missouri R.

■ **Cheyenne River Agency**

Cherry Cr.

Minneconjou Camp ▲

Big Cheyenne R.

■ **Fort Sully**

■ **Pierre**

Lower
Brule
Reservation

Crow
Creek
Reservation

● Agency

North Dakota
South Dakota

North Fork Cheyenne R.

■ **Fort Meade**

BLACK
HILLS

South Fork Cheyenne R.

White R.

Pine Ridge Reservation

Rosebud Reservation

South Fork White R.

● **Rosebud Agency**

Wounded Knee Cr.

Pine Ridge Agency ●

■ **Wounded Knee**

Nebraska

| 0 | 50 | 100 | 150 |

SCALE IN MILES

was sent to the reservation to investigate. Sitting Bull had been released and was living at the Hunkpapa agency at Standing Rock when the commissioners arrived there on August 22. They asked the other chiefs to speak first, deliberately ignoring the most famous living Sioux chief. At last when Senator Dawes came around to him, Sitting Bull showed the commission clearly that he still commanded the Sioux: ". . . you men have come here to talk with us, and you say you do not know who I am. I want to tell you that if the Great Spirit has chosen anyone to be the chief in this country it is myself. . . . You have conducted yourselves like men who have been drinking whiskey, and I came here to give you some advice." He made a sweeping movement with his hand, and every Indian in the council room stood up and followed him out.[3]

Later that day the other Hunkpapa leaders talked with Sitting Bull. They assured him that they were loyal but said that Dawes' commission was not like the land thieves who had come there before. These men wanted to help them keep their land, not take it away from them.

Sitting Bull was not sure that any white people could be trusted, but he offered to apologize for walking out. Instead of listening to what he had to say, the commissioners immediately attacked him. Senator John Logan said: "I want to say further that you are not a great chief of this country, that you have no following, no power, no control, and no right to any control. You are on an Indian reservation merely at the sufferance of the government. You are fed by the government, clothed by the government, your children are educated by the government. If it were not for the government you would be freezing and starving today in the mountains. . . . The government feeds and clothes and educates your children now and desires to teach you to become farmers, and to civilize you, and *make you as white men*."[4]

A strong leader like Sitting Bull threatened the government's policy of making the Sioux over into white men. That is why he was treated as an Indian of no importance. John McLaughlin, the head of Standing Rock agency, dealt with Gall for the Hunkpapas and with John Grass for the Blackfoot Sioux. Every move that McLaughlin made was meant to show the Standing Rock Indians that their old hero was powerless to lead or help them.

But nothing affected Sitting Bull's popularity with the Sioux. All visitors to the reservation, Indian or white, wanted to meet Sitting Bull. In the summer of 1883, when the Northern Pacific Railroad drove the last spike in its track across the continent, Sitting Bull was chosen to speak at the celebration. No other Indian was even considered.

Sitting Bull was to talk in the Sioux language; an interpreter was to translate his words into English. The big event was on September 8 in Bismarck. Sitting Bull was taken to the speakers' platform and introduced. "I hate all the white people," he began. "You are thieves and liars. You have taken away our land and made us outcasts."[5] Knowing that only the interpreter could understand what he was saying, Sitting Bull paused for applause; he bowed, smiled, and then continued his insults. At last he sat down and the bewildered interpreter took his place. By inventing a few friendly sentences and adding some well-worn Indian sayings, he brought the audience to its feet with a standing ovation for Sitting Bull.

The following year, William F. (Buffalo Bill) Cody decided to put the famous chief in his Wild West Show. Crowds flocked to see Sitting Bull. Some booed the "Killer of Custer," but after each show these same people offered him money for copies of his signed photograph. Sitting Bull gave most of it away to the band of ragged, hungry boys who seemed to follow him everywhere.

After the tour ended, he returned to Standing Rock with two farewell presents from Buffalo Bill—a big white sombrero and a performing horse. The horse had been trained to sit down and raise one hoof whenever a gun went off.

In 1887 Buffalo Bill invited Sitting Bull to go with the show on a tour of Europe, but the chief refused. "I am needed here," he said. "There is more talk of taking our lands."[6]

In fact the government was determined to open up the Sioux reservation for settlement, but they did not want to break the treaty of 1868. They hoped the Indians would sell their land out of fear that it would be taken away if they refused to sell.

In 1888 a commission was sent to offer the Indians fifty cents an acre for nine million acres. But they could not get anywhere near the required signatures of three-fourths of the adult males.

Then in May of the following year, a new commission arrived at the Great Sioux Reservation. It was headed by the Indians' old enemy General George Crook. This time the offer was one dollar and fifty cents per acre.

Crook deliberately chose the Rosebud agency for his first council. Spotted Tail had been mysteriously killed by one of his own people eight years earlier; since that time the Brulés had lost their unity and strength. Although there was scattered opposition, a majority of the Brulés finally signed the papers Crook had brought. The first signature was that of Crow Dog, the assassin of Spotted Tail.

At Pine Ridge in June, the commission had to deal with Red Cloud, who showed his power by arriving at the council with hundreds of mounted warriors. Here the commission was only able to get about half of the Oglalas' signatures.

On July 27, after visiting the smaller agencies at Lower Brulé, Crow Creek, and Cheyenne River, the commissioners arrived at Standing Rock. Here the decision would be made. If a majority of the Hunkpapa and Blackfoot Sioux refused to sign, the agreement would fail.

Sitting Bull came to the first councils but remained silent. His presence was all that was needed to create a solid wall of opposition. "The Indians gave close attention," Crook said, "but gave no indication of favor. Their demeanor was rather that of men who had made up their minds and listened from curiosity as to what new arguments could be advanced."[7]

At last Crook realized he would get no signatures in general councils. He asked agent James McLaughlin to help him. McLaughlin's job was to convince individual Indians that the government would simply take their land if they refused to sell.

McLaughlin arranged secret meetings with John Grass, the Blackfoot Sioux leader at Standing Rock. "I talked with him until he agreed that he would speak for its ratification and work for it."[8] Then, without telling Sitting Bull, he scheduled a final meeting with the commissioners on August 3. Indian police were stationed all around to prevent Sitting Bull and his supporters from interrupting, yet they found their way in anyway.

Sitting Bull entered the council circle and began to speak: "I would like to say something unless you object to my speaking, and if you do I will not speak. No one told us of the council, and we just got here."

Crook looked at McLaughlin. "Did Sitting Bull know that we were going to hold a council?" he asked.

"Yes, sir," McLaughlin lied. "Yes, sir, everybody knew it."[9]

At this moment John Grass and the other chiefs moved forward to sign the agreement. It was all over. The Great Sioux Reservation was broken up into small islands. The

white men would soon settle all around them. Before Sitting
Bull could get away, a newspaperman asked him how the
Indians felt about giving up their lands.

"Indians!" shouted Sitting Bull. "There are no Indians left
but me!"

In the Moon of Drying Grass (October 9, 1890), about a year
after the breaking up of the Great Sioux Reservation, a Minneconjou named Kicking Bear came to visit Sitting Bull.
Kicking Bear was just one of several hundred Indians from
different tribes and reservations who had come together far
beyond the Shining Mountains at a place called Walker Lake.
He had just returned from this long journey westward and
he brought news of the Paiute messiah, Wovoka, who had
founded the Ghost Dance religion. Kicking Bear reported
on what he had seen.

For two days the Indians at Walker Lake waited to see
the messiah. Just before sundown, on the third day, he appeared. Kicking Bear had always thought that Christ was
a white man, but this man looked like an Indian. He
spoke to the waiting crowd. "I have sent for you and am
glad to see you. I am going to talk to you after a while about
your relatives who are dead and gone. . . . I will teach you
how to dance a dance, and I want you to dance it." He began
to dance and everyone joined in. Finally, late at night, the
messiah told them they had danced enough.[10]

Next morning, Kicking Bear and the others went up close
to the messiah. They wanted to see if he had the scars of
crucifixion which the missionaries on the reservations had told
them about. There was a scar on his wrist and one on his
face, but they could not see his feet because he was wearing
moccasins. All day long he talked to them. In the beginning, he
said, God made the earth and then sent Christ to teach the

28. *Kicking Bear. Photo by David F. Barry, from the Denver Public Library Western Collection.*

people. But because white men had treated him badly, leaving scars on his body, he had gone back to heaven. Now he had returned to earth as an Indian, and he was to make everything better.

In the next springtime when the grass was high, the earth would be covered with new soil which would bury all the white men. The land would then be covered with sweet flowers and trees and running water. Great herds of buffalo and wild horses would come back. The Indians who danced the Ghost Dance would be kept up in the air until the change was finished. Only Indians would live on the new earth and the ghosts of their dead would return.

Kicking Bear had listened well to the messiah and after returning to the Minneconjou Sioux agency at Cheyenne River, he had started the new dance. His brother, Short Bull, had brought it to the Rosebud, and others had brought it to Pine Ridge.

Sitting Bull thought about all that Kicking Bear had to say about the messiah and the Ghost Dance. Although he did not believe that dead men could live again, his people believed it. They had heard of the messiah and were afraid he would let them die with the white men if they did not dance. Sitting Bull knew that at some agencies soldiers were trying to stop the ceremonies. He did not want soldiers coming in to frighten and perhaps shoot their guns at his people. Kicking Bear told him that if the Indians wore the clothes of the messiah—Ghost Shirts painted with magic symbols—nothing could hurt them. Not even the soldiers' bullets could pierce a Ghost Shirt.

Although he had doubts about the new religion, Sitting Bull invited Kicking Bear to stay at Standing Rock and teach his band the Dance of the Ghosts. At this time it was spreading through the reservations in the West like a prairie fire under a high wind. Government and military authorities were trying hard to understand what was going on. By early autumn the official word was: stop the Ghost Dancing.

None of the white men realized that the new religion taught nonviolence and brotherly love just as Christianity did. "You must not hurt anybody or do harm to anyone. You must not fight. Do right always," said Wovoka. All the Indians had to do was dance and sing. The messiah would bring the new world.

But because the Indians were dancing, the agents became afraid and called the soldiers, and the soldiers began to march.

By mid-November the Ghost Dancing had completely taken over the Sioux agencies. No pupils came to school, no trading was done in the stores, no work was done on the little farms. At Pine Ridge the frightened agent telegraphed Washington: "Indians are dancing in the snow and are wild and crazy. . . . We need protection and we need it now. The leaders should be arrested and confined at some military post until the matter is quieted, and this should be done at once."[11]

On November 20 the Indian Bureau in Washington ordered the agents to send the names of those who had organized the Ghost Dancing. This was the chance James McLaughlin had been waiting for. Now he could get rid of Sitting Bull. He said that the Hunkpapa chief was to blame for the disturbances at Standing Rock.

On December 12 the commanding officer at nearby Fort Yates received orders to capture Sitting Bull. Three days later forty-three Indian policemen surrounded his cabin. Lieutenant Bull Head, the Indian policeman in charge, found Sitting Bull asleep on the floor. "What do you want here?" Sitting Bull asked.

"You are my prisoner," said Bull Head. "You must go to the agency."

Sitting Bull yawned and sat up. "All right," he answered,

"let me put on my clothes and I'll go with you." He asked the policemen to saddle his horse.

When Bull Head came out of the cabin with Sitting Bull, he found a crowd of Ghost Dancers gathering outside. There were many more of them than policemen. Catch-the-Bear, one of the dancers, moved toward Bull Head. "You think you are going to take him," Catch-the-Bear shouted. "You shall not do it." He pulled a rifle from under his blanket and shot Bull Head in the side. As Bull Head fell, he fired, trying to defend himself, but the bullet hit Sitting Bull by mistake. Then another of the Indian police shot Sitting Bull through the head and killed him.

During the shooting, the old performing horse that Buffalo Bill had given Sitting Bull began to go through his tricks. He sat up and raised one hoof. It seemed to onlookers almost as though he was dancing the Ghost Dance. But when the horse stopped and wandered away, the wild fighting began again. Only the arrival of a squadron of cavalry that had been waiting nearby in case of trouble saved the Indian police.[12]

12
Wounded Knee

There was no hope on earth, and God seemed to have forgotten
us. Some said they saw the Son of God; others did not see Him.
If He had come, He would do some great things as He had done
before. We doubted it because we had seen neither Him nor
His works.

The people did not know; they did not care. They snatched
at the hope. They screamed like crazy men to Him for mercy.
They caught at the promise they heard He had made.

The white men were frightened and called for soldiers. We had
begged for life, and the white men thought we wanted theirs.
We heard that soldiers were coming. We did not fear. We hoped
that we could tell them our troubles and get help. A white man
said the soldiers meant to kill us. We did not believe it. . . .

—RED CLOUD

IN THEIR GRIEF and anger over the assassination of Sitting
Bull, the Sioux might have risen up against the soldiers. But
because of the Ghost Dance religion and the belief that the
white men would soon disappear, they did not try to take
revenge.

Many of the Ghost Dancers had left the agencies and
formed camps where they could practice their religion without fear. After the death of Sitting Bull the leaderless Hunkpapas fled Standing Rock and came into these camps for
protection. In the Moon When the Deer Shed Their Horns
(December 17) about a hundred Hunkpapas arrived at a

Minneconjou camp near Cherry Creek. Most of the dancers here were widows who danced until they fainted because they wanted to bring their dead warriors back.

When Big Foot, the head of the camp, learned that Sitting Bull had been killed, he started his people toward Pine Ridge. Red Cloud was the last of the great chiefs. Big Foot hoped Red Cloud would protect them from the soldiers. That same day the War Department ordered Big Foot arrested. He was on the list of leaders responsible for the Ghost Dancing.

On December 28 the Minneconjous saw a large number of soldiers coming. Big Foot had gotten pneumonia and was traveling in a wagon at this time. He immediately ordered a white flag run up.

The Bluecoat commander, Major Samuel Whitside, told Big Foot that he had orders to take him to an army camp on Wounded Knee Creek. The Minneconjou chief answered that he was going in that direction; he was taking his people to Pine Ridge for safety.

Big Foot's blankets were stained with blood; he had begun hemorrhaging. Whitside gave him an army ambulance to ride in. It would be warmer and more comfortable for Big Foot than his springless wagon. After the chief was put in the ambulance, Whitside organized the journey to Wounded Knee Creek. The Indians were herded between soldiers in front and soldiers behind.

It was getting dark when they came over the last hill and began going down toward Chankpe Opi Wakpala, the creek called Wounded Knee. The wintry twilight and the tiny crystals of ice in the air made the landscape appear supernatural. Somewhere along this frozen stream, buried in a secret place, was the heart of Crazy Horse. The Ghost Dancers believed that his spirit was waiting eagerly for the new earth that would surely come in the spring.

29. *Big Foot in death. Photographed at the Wounded Knee battlefield. Courtesy of the Smithsonian Institution.*

At the army camp on Wounded Knee Creek, the Indians were carefully counted. There were 120 men and 230 women and children. Major Whitside's orders were to disarm his prisoners. Because it was almost dark, however, he decided to wait until morning. To make sure none of the Sioux escaped, he placed guards all around. Then he moved two powerful Hotchkiss guns up on a hill. They were pointed at the tepees.

Later that night more soldiers arrived. Colonel James W. Forsyth, commanding Custer's old regiment, now took over. He told Whitside that he had orders to bring Big Foot's band to the Union Pacific Railroad for shipment to a military prison in Omaha.

After putting two more guns on the hill beside the others, Forsyth and his men settled down with a barrel of whiskey to celebrate the capture of Big Foot.

The chief lay in his tent, too ill to sleep, barely able to breathe. Even with their protective Ghost Shirts, his people were afraid of the soldiers camped all around them. Fourteen years before, on the Little Bighorn, some of the warriors had defeated some of these same soldiers. The Indians wondered whether revenge was still in their hearts.

The following morning, Forsyth ordered his men to disarm the Indians. The soldier chiefs were not satisfied with the number of weapons surrendered. They searched the tepees for more. Then they searched each warrior. The Indians' faces showed their anger, but only the medicine man, Yellow Bird, protested openly. He danced a few Ghost Dance steps and chanted in Sioux, "The bullets will not go toward you. The prairie is large and the bullets will not go toward you."[1]

The soldiers found only two rifles; one of them belonged to a young Minneconjou named Black Coyote. Black Coyote raised the rifle above his head, shouting that he had paid much money for it and that it belonged to him. Some years later an Indian who had been present recalled that Black Coyote was deaf. "He hadn't his gun pointed at anyone. His intention was to put that gun down. Right after they spun him around there was the report of a gun, was quite loud. I couldn't say that anybody was shot, but following that was a crash."[2]

Whether or not Black Coyote had meant to shoot his gun, it gave the soldiers a signal to open fire. In the first seconds of violence, the sound of rifles was deafening, and the air was filled with powder smoke. Among the dying who lay sprawled on the frozen ground was Big Foot. There was a short pause in the sound of arms while small groups of Indians and soldiers fought each other with knives, clubs, and pistol butts. But because most of the Indians had no weapons, they soon had to flee. Then the four big guns on the hill opened up on them, shredding the tepees with flying shrapnel, killing men, women, and children.

"We tried to run," Louise Weasel Bear said, "but they shot us like we were a buffalo. I know there are some good white people, but the soldiers must be mean to shoot children and women. Indian soldiers would not do that to white children."[3]

When the madness ended, Big Foot and more than half of his people were dead or seriously wounded. One estimate was that nearly three hundred of the original three hundred and fifty men, women, and children had been killed.

Later that day, some soldiers went over the Wounded Knee battlefield. They gathered up all the Indians who were still alive and loaded them into wagons. Because a blizzard was approaching, the dead Indians were left lying where they had fallen. (After the blizzard, when a burial party returned to Wounded Knee they found the bodies, including Big Foot's, frozen into grotesque shapes.)

The wagonloads of wounded Sioux included four men and forty-seven women and children. They arrived at Pine Ridge after dark. Because the barracks were filled with soldiers, the Indians were left lying in the open wagons in the bitter cold while an army officer searched for shelter. Finally the Episcopal mission was opened, the benches taken out, and hay scattered over the rough floor.

It was the fourth day after Christmas in the year 1890 when the first torn and bleeding bodies were carried into the candlelit church. Those who were conscious could see Christmas greenery hanging from the open rafters.

Above the pulpit was strung a crudely lettered banner: PEACE ON EARTH, GOOD WILL TO MEN.

30. *"They made us many promises, more than I can remember, but they never kept but one; they promised to take our land, and they took it."* Reproduced from the collections of the Library of Congress. Photograph by E. S. Curtis.

Indian Moons

AMERICAN INDIAN CALENDARS differed from tribe to tribe. Some tribes simply divided the year into four or five seasons, while others divided it into periods which began with each new moon. Their choice of name for a moon was usually based upon the world of nature—animals, birds, plants, weather. The moon names often indicated whether a tribe depended upon hunting or agriculture for its subsistence. They also revealed something of the climate where a particular tribe lived.

As each moon cycle lasts for about twenty-eight days, Indian moons do not correspond exactly with our months. For example, an Indian moon may overlap from December into January, from January into February, and so on, for a total of thirteen moons in each year.

These are some Indian moons listed by the months in which they usually occur:

JANUARY

Sioux:	Moon of Strong Cold
Zuñi:	Moon When the Limbs of Trees Are Broken by Snow
Omaha:	Moon When the Snow Drifts into the Tepees
Tewa Pueblo:	Ice Moon
Cherokee:	Windy Moon

FEBRUARY

Sioux:	Raccoon Moon
Omaha:	Moon When the Geese Come Home

Tewa Pueblo: Moon of the Cedar Dust Wind
Kiowa: Little Bud Moon
Winnebago: Fish-Running Moon

MARCH

Sioux: Moon When the Buffalo Cows Drop Their
                        Calves
Omaha: Little Frog Moon
Tewa Pueblo: Moon When the Leaves Break Forth
Cherokee: Strawberry Moon
Ponca: Water Stands in the Ponds Moon

APRIL

Sioux: Moon of Greening Grass
Cheyenne: Moon When the Geese Lay Eggs
Winnebago: Planting-Corn Moon
Kiowa: Leaf Moon
Mandan-Hidatsa: Moon of the Breaking Up of the Ice

MAY

Sioux: Moon When the Ponies Shed
Creek: Mulberry Moon
Osage: Moon When the Little Flowers Die
Cheyenne: Moon When the Horses Get Fat
Winnebago: Hoeing-Corn Moon

JUNE

Sioux: Moon of Making Fat
Omaha: Moon When the Buffalo Bulls Hunt the
                        Cows
Tewa Pueblo: Moon When the Leaves Are Dark Green
Ponca: Hot Weather Begins Moon
Winnebago: Corn-Tasseling Moon

JULY

Sioux:	Moon When the Wild Cherries Are Ripe
Omaha:	Moon When the Buffalo Bellow
Kiowa:	Moon of Deer Horns Dropping Off
Creek:	Little Ripening Moon
Winnebago:	Corn-Popping Moon

AUGUST

Sioux:	Moon When the Geese Shed Their Feathers
Cherokee:	Drying Up Moon
Ponca:	Corn Is in the Silk Moon
Creek:	Big Ripening Moon
Osage:	Yellow Flower Moon

SEPTEMBER

Sioux:	Moon of Drying Grass
Omaha:	Moon When the Deer Paw the Earth
Tewa Pueblo:	Moon When the Corn Is Taken In
Cherokee:	Black Butterfly Moon
Creek:	Little Chestnut Moon

OCTOBER

Sioux:	Moon of Falling Leaves
Zuñi:	Big Wind Moon
Ponca:	Moon When They Store Food in Caches
Cheyenne:	Moon When the Water Begins to Freeze on the Edge of Streams
Kiowa:	Ten-Colds Moon

NOVEMBER

Creek:	Moon When the Water Is Black with Leaves
Kiowa:	Geese-Going Moon

Mandan-Hidatsa: Moon When the Rivers Freeze
Tewa Pueblo: Moon When All Is Gathered In
Winnebago: Little Bear's Moon

DECEMBER

Sioux: Moon of Popping Trees
Cheyenne: Moon When the Wolves Run Together
Creek: Big Winter Moon
Arikara: Moon of the Nose of the Great Serpent
Winnebago: Big Bear's Moon

Notes

Chapter 1:   THE LONG WALK OF THE NAVAHOS

1 U.S. Congress. 49th. 1st session. House of Representatives
Executive Document 263, p. 14.
2 U.S. Congress. 39th. 2nd session. Senate Report 156, p. 314.
3 *Ibid.*, p. 139.
4 U.S. Congress. 49th. 1st session. House of Representatives
Executive Document 263, p. 15.
5 Senate Report 156, pp. 144, 157, 162–67, 174, 179, 183–84,
259–60. Lynn R. Bailey, *Long Walk* (Los Angeles: Westernlore, 1964), pp. 164–66. Document in Lawrence C. Kelly,
Navajo Roundup (Boulder: Pruett, 1970). William A. Kelle-
her, *Turmoil in New Mexico, 1846–1868* (Santa Fe: Rydal
Press, 1952), p. 441.
6 Senate Report 156, pp. 221–22.
7 U.S. Office of Indian Affairs. Report, 1867, p. 190.
8 House of Representatives Executive Document 263, p. 15.

Chapter 2:   COCHISE AND THE APACHE GUERRILLAS

1 Daniel E. Connor, *Joseph Reddeford Walker and the Arizona
Adventure* (Norman: University of Oklahoma Press, 1956),
p. 37.
2 *Ibid.*, pp. 38–42.
3 U.S. Secretary of the Interior. Report, 1871, p. 486.
4 *Ibid.*, p. 470.
5 A. N. Ellis, "Recollections of an Interview with Cochise, Chief
of the Apaches." Kansas State Historical Society, *Collections*,
Vol. 13, 1915, pp. 391–92.
6 O. O. Howard, *My Life and Experiences Among Our Hostile*

Indians (Hartford: A. D. Worthington and Co., 1907), pp. 204–19.

7 Woodworth Clum, *Apache Agent, The Story of John P. Clum* (Boston: Houghton Mifflin, 1936), pp. 99–100, 129.

8 Frank C. Lockwood, *Pioneer Days in Arizona* (New York: Macmillan, 1932), pp. 171–72.

Chapter 3: THE LAST OF THE APACHE CHIEFS

1 Britton Davis, *The Truth About Geronimo* (Chicago: Lakeside Press, 1951), p. 48.

2 U.S. Secretary of War. Report, 1883, pp. 159–65.

3 *Ibid.*, p. 167.

4 Dan L. Thrapp, *The Conquest of Apacheria* (Norman: University of Oklahoma Press, 1967), p. 290.

5 John G. Bourke, *An Apache Campaign in the Sierra Madre* (New York: Charles Scribner's Sons, 1958), p. 114.

6 U.S. Congress. 51st. 1st session. Senate Executive Document 88, pp. 16–17.

7 S. M. Barrett, *Geronimo's Story of His Life* (New York: Duffield & Company, 1907), p. 139.

8 Odie B. Faulk, *The Geronimo Campaign* (New York: Oxford University Press, 1969), pp. 125–26.

Chapter 4: WAR COMES TO THE CHEYENNES

1 George Bird Grinnell, *The Fighting Cheyennes* (Norman: University of Oklahoma Press, 1956), pp. 145–46.

2 Donald J. Berthrong, *The Southern Cheyennes* (Norman: University of Oklahoma Press, 1963), p. 185.

3 U.S. Congress. 39th. 2nd session. Senate Report 156, p. 94.

4 *Ibid.*, pp. 55–56.

5 U.S. Secretary of the Interior. Report, 1864, pp. 374–75.

6 Stan Hoig, *The Sand Creek Massacre* (Norman: University of Oklahoma Press, 1961), p. 99.

7 U.S. Congress. 39th. 2nd session. Senate Executive Document 26, p. 44.

8 Senate Report 156, p. 77.

9 *Ibid., pp.* 87–90.

10 George E. Hyde, *Life of George Bent* (Norman: University of Oklahoma Press, 1968), p. 146.

11 U.S. Congress. 38th. 2nd session. Senate Report 142, p. 18.

12 Senate Executive Document 26, p. 25.

13 George Bent to George E. Hyde, April 14, 1906. Coe Collection, Yale University.

14 Senate Executive Document 26, p. 70.

15 Senate Report 156, pp. 73, 96.

16 George Bent, "Forty Years with the Cheyennes." *The Frontier*, Vol. IV, No. 6, December 1905, p. 3.

17 U.S. Secretary of the Interior. Report, 1865, pp. 701–11.

Chapter 5: POWDER RIVER INVASION

1 George Bent, "Forty Years with the Cheyennes." *The Frontier*, Vol. IV, No. 7, January 1906, p. 4.

2 Official Record. *The War of the Rebellion*, Series I, Vol. 48, Pt. 2, pp. 1048–49.

3 George Bird Grinnell, *The Fighting Cheyennes* (Norman: University of Oklahoma Press, 1956), pp. 210–11.

4 H. E. Palmer, "History of the Powder River Indian Expedition of 1865." Nebraska State Historical Society, *Transactions and Reports*, Vol. II, p. 216.

5 George E. Hyde, *Life of George Bent* (Norman: University of Oklahoma Press, 1968), pp. 239–40.

Chapter 6: RED CLOUD'S WAR

1 U.S. Department of the Interior. Report, 1866, pp. 206–7.

2 U.S. Congress. 50th. 1st session. Senate Executive Document 33, p. 5.

3 Margaret I. Carrington, *Ab-sa-ra-ka, Land of Massacre* (Philadelphia: Lippincott, 1878), pp. 79–80.

4 John Stands in Timber and Margot Liberty, *Cheyenne Memories* (New Haven: Yale University Press, 1967), p. 172.

5 *Ibid.*, pp. 174–76.

6 John G. Neihardt, *Black Elk Speaks* (Lincoln: University of Nebraska Press, 1961), p. 17.

7 Henry M. Stanley, *My Early Travels and Adventures* (New York: Scribner's, 1895), Vol. I, pp. 201–16.

8 U.S. Congress. 40th. 2nd session. House Executive Document 97, p. 5.

9 *Omaha Weekly Herald,* June 10, 1868.

Chapter 7: "THE ONLY GOOD INDIAN IS A DEAD INDIAN"

1 U.S. Secretary of the Interior. Report, 1867, p. 311.

2 Henry M. Stanley, *My Early Travels and Adventures* (New York: Scribner's, 1895), Vol. 1, pp. 37–38. George B. Grinnell, *The Fighting Cheyennes* (Norman: University of Oklahoma Press, 1956), pp. 250–52.

3 U.S. Congress. 40th. 1st session. Senate Executive Document 13, p. 95.

4 Charles J. Brill, *Conquest of the Southern Plains* (Oklahoma City: 1938), p. 107.

5 Grinnell, p. 286.

6 De Benneville Randolph Keim, *Sheridan's Troopers on the Borders* (Philadelphia: McKay, 1885), p. 103.

7 Donald J. Berthrong, *The Southern Cheyennes* (Norman: University of Oklahoma Press, 1963), p. 332.

8 Sheridan Papers, January 1, 1869, as quoted in Berthrong, pp. 333–34.

9 Edward S. Ellis, *The History of Our Country* (Indianapolis: J. H. Woolling and Co., 1900), Vol. 6, p. 1483.

Chapter 8:   RED CLOUD'S VISIT TO WASHINGTON

1 U.S. Department of the Interior. Report, 1870, pp. 672–82.

2 U.S. Congress. 41st. 3rd session. Senate Executive Document 39, pp. 38–39.

3 *Ibid.,* p. 39.

4 *Ibid.,* pp. 40–41.

5 *Ibid.,* pp. 42–44.

6 *The New York Times,* June 17, 1870.

7 James C. Olson, *Red Cloud and the Sioux Problem* (Lincoln: University of Nebraska Press, 1965), p. 127.

Chapter 9:   THE WAR FOR THE BLACK HILLS

1 Hila Gilbert, *"Big Bat" Pourier* (Sheridan, Wyoming: Mills Company, 1968), p. 43.
2 Anson Mills, *My Story* (Washington, D.C.: 1918), p. 168.
3 U.S. Commissioner of Indian Affairs. Report, 1875, p. 199.
4 U.S. Congress. 44th. 1st session. House Executive Document 184, p. 10.
5 John G. Neihardt, *Black Elk Speaks* (Lincoln: University of Nebraska Press, 1961), p. 90.
6 Thomas B. Marquis, *Wooden Leg, A Warrior Who Fought Custer* (Lincoln: University of Nebraska Press, 1957), p. 168.
7 Hamlin Garland, "General Custer's Last Fight as Seen by Two Moon." *McClure's Magazine,* Vol. 11, 1898, p. 445.
8 Stanley Vestal, *Sitting Bull, Champion of the Sioux* (Norman: University of Oklahoma Press, 1957), pp. 150–51.
9 Neihardt, p. 106.
10 Marquis, p. 205.
11 James McLaughlin, *My Friend the Indian* (Boston: Houghton Mifflin Co., 1910), pp. 168–69.
12 Neihardt, pp. 108–9.
13 Garland, p. 446.
14 New York *Herald,* September 24, 1876.
15 McLaughlin, p. 175.
16 New York *Herald,* November 16, 1877.
17 U.S. Congress. 44th. 2nd session. Senate Executive Document 9, p. 5.
18 New York *Herald,* September 23, 1876.
19 Senate Executive Document 9, p. 66.
20 U.S. Secretary of the Interior. Report, 1877, p. 724.

Chapter 10:   CHEYENNE EXODUS

1 Thomas B. Marquis, *Wooden Leg, A Warrior Who Fought Custer* (Lincoln: University of Nebraska Press, 1957), p. 310.
2 *Ibid.,* p. 320.
3 U.S. Congress. 46th. 2nd session. Senate Report 708, pp. 153, 266, 269.
4 *Ibid.,* p. 278.

5 Edgar B. Bronson, *Reminiscences of a Ranchman* (New York: McClure Company, 1908), pp. 167–69.
6 Senate Report 708, p. 244.
7 "Liquidation of Dull Knife." *Nebraska History*, Vol. 22, 1941, pp. 109–10.
8 Senate Report 708, p. 242.
9 *Ibid.*, p. 249.
10 Marquis, p. 333.

Chapter 11:   DANCE OF THE GHOSTS

1 U.S. Secretary of the Interior. Report, 1877, pp. 726–27.
2 John G. Neihardt, *Black Elk Speaks* (Lincoln: University of Nebraska Press, 1961), p. 159.
3 U.S. Congress. 48th. 1st session. Senate Report 283, pp. 71–72.
4 *Ibid.*, pp. 79–81.
5 Kate E. Glaspell, "Incidents in the Life of the Pioneer." *North Dakota Historical Quarterly*, Vol. 8, 1941, pp. 187–88.
6 Stanley Vestal, *Sitting Bull, Champion of the Sioux* (Norman: University of Oklahoma Press, 1957), p. 255.
7 U.S. Congress. 51st. 1st session. Senate Executive Document 51, p. 21.
8 James McLaughlin, *My Friend the Indian* (Boston: Houghton Mifflin Co., 1910), p. 285.
9 Senate Executive Document 51, p. 213.
10 U.S. Bureau of Ethnology. Report, 14th, 1892–93, Pt. 2, p. 795.
11 James C. Olson, *Red Cloud and the Sioux Problem* (Lincoln: University of Nebraska Press, 1965), p. 326.
12 Martin F. Schmitt and Dee Brown, *Fighting Indians of the West* (New York: Charles Scribner's Sons, 1958), p. 335.

Chapter 12:   WOUNDED KNEE

1 Robert M. Utley, *The Last Days of the Sioux Nation* (New Haven: Yale University Press, 1963), p. 210.
2 James H. McGregor, *The Wounded Knee Massacre from the Viewpoint of the Survivors* (Baltimore: Wirth Brothers, 1940), p. 106.
3 *Ibid.*, p. 111.

Bibliography

Andrist, Ralph K., *The Long Death: The Last Days of the Plains Indian.* New York, Macmillan, 1964.

Bailey, Lynn R., *Long Walk.* Los Angeles, Westernlore, 1964.

Beal, Merrill D., *"I Will Fight No More Forever": Chief Joseph and the Nez Percé War.* Seattle, University of Washington Press, 1963.

Berthrong, Donald J., *The Southern Cheyennes.* Norman, University of Oklahoma Press, 1963.

Betzincz, Jason, and Nye, W. S., *I Fought with Geronimo.* Harrisburg, Pa., Stackpole, 1960.

Bourke, John G., *An Apache Campaign in the Sierra Madre.* New York, Charles Scribner's Sons, 1958.

Britt, Albert, *Great Indian Chiefs.* New York, Whittlesey House, 1938.

Brown, Dee, *Fort Phil Kearny: An American Saga.* New York, Putnam's, 1962.

Carley, Kenneth. *The Sioux Uprising of 1862.* St. Paul, Minnesota Historical Society, 1961.

Carter, R. G., *On the Border with Mackenzie.* New York, Antiquarian Press, 1961.

Clum, Woodworth, *Apache Agent: The Story of John P. Clum.* Boston, Houghton Mifflin, 1936.

Crook, George, *Autobiography,* Martin F. Schmitt, ed. Norman, University of Oklahoma Press, 1946.

Davis, Britton, *The Truth About Geronimo.* Chicago, Lakeside Press, 1951.

DeBarthe, Joe, *Life and Adventures of Frank Grouard.* Norman, University of Oklahoma Press, 1958.

Emmit, Robert, *The Last War Trail: The Utes and the Settlement of Colorado*. Norman, University of Oklahoma Press, 1954.

Ewers, John C., *Indian Life of the Upper Missouri*. Norman, University of Oklahoma Press, 1968.

Falk, Odie B., *The Geronimo Campaign*. New York, Oxford University Press, 1969.

Finerty, John F., *Warpath and Bivouac*. Chicago, Lakeside Press, 1955.

Fritz, Henry E., *The Movement for Indian Assimilation, 1860–1890*. Philadelphia, University of Pennsylvania Press, 1963.

Graham, W. A., *The Custer Myth*. Harrisburg, Pa., Stackpole, 1953.

Grinnell, George B., *The Fighting Cheyennes*. Norman, University of Oklahoma Press, 1956.

Hafen, Le Roy R. and Ann W., *Powder River Campaigns and Sawyers' Expedition of 1865*. Glendale, Calif., A. H. Clark, 1961.

Hoig, Stan, *The Sand Creek Massacre*. Norman, University of Oklahoma Press, 1961.

Howard, James H., *The Ponca Tribe* (Bureau of American Ethnology Bulletin 195), Washington, D.C., 1965.

Hyde, George E., *Life of George Bent*, written from his letters, Savoie Lottinville, ed. Norman, University of Oklahoma Press, 1967.

————, *Red Cloud's Folk: A History of the Oglala Sioux Indians*. Norman, University of Oklahoma Press, 1937.

————, *A Sioux Chronicle*. Norman, University of Oklahoma Press, 1956.

————, *Spotted Tail's Folk: A History of the Brulé Sioux*. Norman, University of Oklahoma Press, 1961.

Jackson, Donald, *Custer's Gold: The United States Cavalry Expedition of 1874*. New Haven, Yale University Press, 1966.

John Stands in Timber and Margot Liberty, *Cheyenne Memories*. New Haven, Yale University Press, 1967.

Jones, Douglas C., *The Treaty of Medicine Lodge*. Norman, University of Oklahoma Press, 1966.

Josephy, Alvin M., Jr., *The Nez Percé Indians and the Opening of the Northwest*. New Haven, Yale University Press, 1965.

Lavender, David, *Bent's Fort*. New York, Doubleday, 1954.

Leckie, William H., *The Military Conquest of the Southern Plains*. Norman, University of Oklahoma Press, 1963.

McGregor, James H., *The Wounded Knee Massacre from the Viewpoint of the Survivors*. Baltimore, Wirth Bros., 1940.

Marquis, Thomas B., *Wooden Leg: A Warrior Who Fought Custer*. Lincoln, University of Nebraska Press, 1957.

Marriott, Alice, *The Ten Grandmothers*. Norman, University of Oklahoma Press, 1945.

Mayhall, Mildred P., *The Kiowas*. Norman, University of Oklahoma Press, 1962.

Meyer, Roy W., *History of the Santee Sioux*. Lincoln, University of Nebraska Press, 1967.

Murray, Keith A., *The Modocs and Their War*. Norman, University of Oklahoma Press, 1959.

Neihardt, John G., *Black Elk Speaks*. Lincoln, University of Nebraska Press, 1961.

Oehler, C. M., *The Great Sioux Uprising*. New York, Oxford University Press, 1959.

Olson, James C., *Red Cloud and the Sioux Problem*. Lincoln, University of Nebraska Press, 1965.

A *Pictographic History of the Oglala Sioux*, drawings by Amos Bad Heart Bull, text by Helen H. Blish. Lincoln, University of Nebraska Press, 1967.

Praus, Alexis A., *A New Pictographic Autobiography of Sitting Bull* (Smithsonian Miscellaneous Collections, Vol. 123, No. 6). Washington, D.C., 1955.

Sandoz, Mari, *Cheyenne Autumn*. New York, Hastings House, 1953.

———, *Crazy Horse: The Strange Man of the Oglalas*. New York, Knopf, 1945.

———, *Hostiles and Friendlies*. Lincoln, University of Nebraska Press, 1959.

Schellie, Don, *Vast Domain of Blood: The Camp Grant Massacre*. Los Angeles, Westernlore, 1968.

Schmitt, Martin F., and Brown, Dee, *Fighting Indians of the West*. New York, Charles Scribner's Sons, 1948.

Sonnichsen, C. L., *The Mescalero Apaches*. Norman, University of Oklahoma Press, 1958.

Sprague, Marshall, *Massacre: The Tragedy at White River*. Boston, Little, Brown, 1957.

Stewart, Edgar I., *Custer's Luck*. Norman, University of Oklahoma Press, 1955.

Stirling, M. W., *Three Pictographic Autobiographies of Sitting Bull* (Smithsonian Miscellaneous Collections, Vol. 97, No. 5). Washington, D.C., 1938.

Swanton, John R., *The Indian Tribes of North America*. Washington, D.C., 1952.

Thrapp, Dan L., *The Conquest of Apacheria*. Norman, University of Oklahoma Press, 1967.

Tibbles, Thomas Henry, *Buckskin and Blanket Days*. New York, Doubleday, 1957.

Utley, Robert M., *Custer and the Great Controversy*. Los Angeles, Westernlore, 1962.

———, *Frontiersmen in Blue: The U.S. Army and the Indian, 1848–1865*. New York, Macmillan, 1967.

———, *The Last Days of the Sioux Nation*. New Haven, Yale University Press, 1963.

Vaughn, J. W., *The Battle of Platte Bridge*. Norman, University of Oklahoma Press, 1964.

———, *The Reynolds Campaign on Powder River*. Norman, University of Oklahoma Press, 1961.

———, *With Crook at the Rosebud*. Harrisburg, Pa., Stackpole, 1956.

Vestal, Stanley, *Sitting Bull, Champion of the Sioux*. Norman, University of Oklahoma Press, 1957.

Wallace, Ernest, and Hoebel, E. Adamson, *The Comanches, Lords of the South Plains*. Norman, University of Oklahoma Press, 1952.

Ware, Eugene F., *The Indian War of 1864*. New York, St. Martin's Press, 1960.

White Bull, Joseph, *The Warrior Who Killed Custer . . .* , James H. Howard, trans. and ed. Lincoln, University of Nebraska Press, 1968.

Index

DEE BROWN is the author of sixteen books on Western American history, the most recent of which is *The Westerners*. For several years he was a librarian at the University of Illinois. He makes his home in Urbana, Illinois.

AMY EHRLICH was a children's book editor before leaving publishing to free lance. The author of *Zeek Silver Moon*, a picture book, she is presently living in southern Vermont with her family.